QUIET AT SCHOOL

QUIET AT SCHOOL

An Educator's Guide
to Shy Children

**ROBERT J. COPLAN and
KATHLEEN MORITZ RUDASILL**

Foreword by Sandee McClowry

TEACHERS COLLEGE PRESS

TEACHERS COLLEGE | COLUMBIA UNIVERSITY

NEW YORK AND LONDON

Published by Teachers College Press, 1234 Amsterdam Avenue, New York, NY
10027

Cover design by adam b. bohannon.
Cover photo by Zeynep Özyürek for iStock by Getty Images.

Library of Congress Cataloging-in-Publication Data

Names: Coplan, Robert J., 1967- author. | Rudasill, Kathleen Moritz, author.
Title: Quiet at school : an educator's guide to shy children / Robert J. Coplan,
    Kathleen Moritz Rudasill.
Description: New York, NY : Teachers College Press, 2016. | Includes
    bibliographical references and index.
Identifiers: LCCN 2015046221
ISBN 9780807757697 (pbk. : alk. paper)
ISBN 9780807757703 (hardcover : alk. paper)
ISBN 9780807774816 (ebook)
Subjects: LCSH: Children with social disabilities—Education. | Bashfulness in
    children. | Social interaction in children.
Classification: LCC LC4065 .C67 2016 | DDC 371.94—dc23
LC record available at http://lccn.loc.gov/2015046221

ISBN 978-0-8077-5769-7 (paper)
ISBN 978-0-8077-5770-3 (hardcover)
ISBN 978-0-8077-7481-6 (ebook)

Printed on acid-free paper
Manufactured in the United States of America

23 22 21 20 19 18 17 16   8 7 6 5 4 3 2 1

To our families . . . our most important teachers.
                    —*Rob Coplan & Kathy Rudasill*

Contents

Foreword

Imagine for a moment a shy child coming into your classroom for the first time. If you could perceive that first day through the eyes of your shy student, you would understand the high level of discomfort the child experiences in a new environment surrounded by unfamiliar classmates and adults. While other students are focused on what you are saying, your shy student's attention is diverted by worrying about being called upon to speak in front of the whole class. Within a few weeks, however, you notice that your shy student has a new best friend, responds less tentatively to your requests, and occasionally volunteers to answer a question you pose to the class.

In a different classroom in your school, another shy student is exhibiting symptoms of anxiety after a few weeks. The child frequently complains of tummy and headaches, does not easily engage with classmates on the playground, and looks even more frightened when asked to participate in class discussions. Both students have temperaments that are "shy." However, although they began the school year with a great deal of trepidation, these two students display very different levels of comfort and engagement after several weeks. What accounts for the changes in one student compared to the other? More than likely, your responsive teacher strategies made all the difference. Perhaps you applied some of the practices you learned about in this engaging book!

Results from multiple research studies have shown that the academic skills of shy children are often underestimated by their teachers. Shy children hesitate to respond, even when they know the answer. Their self-consciousness causes them to second-guess what they do know. Instead, they expend negative energy that distracts them from learning and from successfully engaging with their classmates and with you. And yet, the sensitivity that shy children possess can be an asset. They often are highly skilled at identifying the nuances of the environment and at reading the emotions of their classmates and the adults who teach and care for them. Rather than trying to change shy students to behave more like their outgoing peers, this book will teach you to capitalize on their strengths so that they can better cope with their natural reticence.

As the developer of an evidence-based intervention, *INSIGHTS into Children's Temperament*, I have had many opportunities to interact with shy children and the teachers who are challenged to meet their needs. The teacher practices described in the book are not pulled from a bag of tricks. They are grounded in temperament theory, research, and what the authors have learned by working directly with children.

Quiet at School: An Educator's Guide to Shy Children is one of those rare books that builds on something that you, as a teacher, already know: Each child in your classroom has a unique set of attributes that contribute to his or her emotional, behavioral, and academic growth. This book begins by updating you on the fascinating research that explains why some of your students are more shy than others. The authors also present quirky scientific facts about shy children that will amuse you. Then, based on the empirical evidence, they jam-pack the book with practical advice for supporting and engaging shy students "one small step at a time." The recommended practices will also help you straddle the thin line between being responsive and reacting over-protectively—which only serves to make shy children even more anxious.

Rob Coplan and Kathy Rudasill are unique leaders in the temperament field. For more than 2 decades, their research has influenced practitioners and researchers alike. Now you and I can benefit from the evidence-based teacher practices they offer throughout this book. Actually, the ones who will benefit the most are the shy children who sit quietly in your classroom.

—Sandee McClowry, PhD, RN, FAAN;
professor, Counseling Psychology and Teaching & Learning,
New York University;
developer, *INSIGHTS into Children's Temperament*

Preface

It is a common experience for many children to feel somewhat wary or nervous when meeting unfamiliar people or to feel self-conscious or embarrassed when they are thrust into the center of attention. Indeed, over 80% of adults report they are or have been shy at some point in their lives! But for extremely shy children, everyday tasks at school—like speaking up in class, working on a group project, or playing with other children at recess—can be sources of significant stress and anxiety.

Yet, shy children have historically been largely ignored in school settings, particularly as compared to their peers who display acting-out problems like bullying or inattention. The reasons for this are not hard to fathom. In short, the squeaky wheel gets the grease! Children who are bouncing off the walls, hurting others, or disrupting the learning environment demand our immediate and repeated attention. In contrast, shy and quiet children are more likely to avoid our attention. Indeed, in the past, psychologists have suggested that teachers might encourage shy behaviors because they maintain order in the classroom.

The last 25 years have been witness to a huge increase in research related to the development and implications of childhood shyness. However, shy children are still not well understood by many teachers and school personnel. For example, shy children tend to go unnoticed in typical classrooms because of their quiet natures. And when they do get noticed, teachers may misattribute shy children's lack of verbal participation in class as evidence of lower intelligence, learning difficulties, or a lack of academic motivation.

This book is intended to help elementary school educators build better awareness of shyness in their classrooms and to integrate best practices for helping shy children thrive at school. Although our primary focus ranges from children in kindergarten to Grade 8, educators of both younger and older children will still find valuable insights in this book. Here is how we have organized the contents:

Chapter 1 explores the basic question of *what is shyness?* We introduce the concept of shyness, provide an overview of how our understanding of this phenomenon has developed, discuss in detail the main components that help define what shyness is, and differentiate shyness from other related but distinct concepts. The next two chapters focus on *how shyness develops.* In

Chapter 2 we examine the effects of nature, exploring the biological and genetic foundations of shyness and its development from an evolutionary perspective. Chapter 3 considers the effects of nurture, with a look at how parents respond to their shy children and socialization practices that might be particularly helpful or harmful for shy children.

In Chapter 4 we consider the potential implications of shyness for children. Here we take a closer look at how shyness might impact children's social, emotional, and academic development—highlighting both the potential *costs and benefits of shyness*. Chapter 5 considers the experiences of *shy children in the classroom*. We discuss why the classroom might be particularly stressful for shy children and how shyness may influence children's academic development. In Chapter 6, we focus specifically on *shy children and teachers*. Topics include how teachers typically react and respond to shy children in their classrooms and the different types of relationships that teachers may form with shy children.

The next two chapters are devoted to *best practices for teachers* for helping shy children to cope successfully with the unique challenges that they face at school. First, in Chapter 7 we review general psychological principles that can be adapted and applied by educators in their interactions with shy children (e.g., graduated exposure, cognitive-behavioral approaches, relaxation techniques). Then, Chapter 8 describes more specific strategies for teachers to assist shy children in challenging situations at school (e.g., facilitating the transition to school, increasing participation in classroom activities, optimizing testing situations). Finally, in Chapter 9, we first take some time to *look back* at the most important points from each of the previous chapters. Then we spend some time *looking forward*, speculating about how our rapidly changing society (e.g., technological advances, increasing cultural diversity) might impact upon the future development and implications of shyness at school.

All of this information is derived and synthesized from the latest research in educational and developmental psychology. In short, this book gathers together everything teachers should know about shy children at school!

CHAPTER 1

What Is Shyness?

CASE STUDY 1.1: KINDERGARTEN

When the bell rings to go inside on the first day of kindergarten, Daniel cries and clings to his mother. Even after all the rest of the children have settled into their morning routine, he will not leave his mother's side.

CASE STUDY 1.2: GRADE 2

Ava does not volunteer to speak in her Grade 2 class. When questioned directly by the teacher, she avoids eye contact and either whispers or does not respond at all.

CASE STUDY 1.3: GRADE 4

During recess time in the schoolyard, a large and boisterous group of Grade 4 children are kicking around a soccer ball and talking animatedly. Off to the side, Noah stands quietly by himself, shoulders hunched over, watching intently but making no attempt to join in.

CASE STUDY 1.4: GRADE 7

While presenting her book report in front of her Grade 7 class, Emma develops a splotchy rash on her face and neck. Although her eyes never leave her cue cards, she loses her place in her notes on several occasions and becomes quite flustered. She finally just stops talking and returns to her seat without completing her presentation.

Most teachers would not have a particularly hard time describing how shy children typically behave in their class. Even very young children are quite good at this, citing examples such as "does not talk," "turns red in the face," and "plays alone" as characteristics of their shy classmates. Many people would probably use these exemplar behaviors as a way to define shyness ("I know it when I see it")—applying the principle illustrated in an expression made popular in the movie Forrest Gump: *shyness is what shyness does* (you are what you do). However, providing an explicit and all-encompassing definition for shyness turns out to be quite complicated—and remains an ongoing challenge for developmental psychologists!

Shyness has been described as a *fuzzy* term because it can mean different things to different people. One reason why shyness is particularly complicated to define is because it involves emotions and behaviors that are not, in and of themselves, indicative of or unique to shyness. For example, shy children tend to be *socially withdrawn,* often removing themselves from opportunities for social interaction and remaining off by themselves in the presence of peers. However, children may play alone for many different reasons that have nothing to do with being shy (for example, some children just prefer solitary play).

Another reason why shyness is hard to define is because it can refer to both a state and a trait. A *state* is how you are feeling at any given time or in any particular situation. States are context-based, shorter term, and prone to change. For example, most children (and adults too!) would report feeling shy (at least to some degree) when called on to give a speech in front of the class. Similarly, most teenagers (and adults too!) would report similar feelings of shyness when going out on a first date. This helps us to understand why so many people might identify themselves as being or having been shy. Many, if not most, of us feel at least somewhat shy sometimes and in some situations. However, these emotions would be tied to these specific situations and would not typically last very long or carry over to other settings.

In contrast, a *trait* refers to an enduring aspect of personality. Traits are quite stable, persisting over time and across situations. As well, traits are thought to exhibit considerable influence over our emotions, thoughts, motivations, and behaviors. To further complicate matters, individuals differ in the amount, level, or degree of each trait. That is to say, traits do not have a specific cutoff point—they are not either present or absent in people. For example, it is not simply the case that we can classify some children as *shy* and the rest as *not shy*. Instead, all children would have greater or lesser *degrees* of shyness and all other traits.

Most individuals tend to score about average on a given trait as compared to everyone else. For example, imagine that we observed 100 different children on the playground at school and assigned each of them a shyness rating from 1 (not at all shy) to 10 (extremely shy). Most children (probably over half) would have scores in the middle of this range (i.e., ratings of 4, 5, or 6). A small group (about 15%) would tend to score right near the bottom of the scale (i.e., ratings of 1 or 2). We might label these children as outgoing, bold, or sociable, but the decision as to where to make this cutoff can be pretty arbitrary (what about a child who scored a rating of 3?). Another small group (also about 15%) would score right at the top of this scale (i.e., ratings of 9 or 10). We would likely label these children as extremely shy (but again, the exact cutoff point remains quite arbitrary).

Someone who is very high on the *trait* of shyness would feel very shy across time and in many situations. For these children, shyness would be more consistently manifested at school in a number of important and influential ways. However, it is important to note that children who scored lower in shyness on this scale would also show signs of shyness at school (although presumably to a lesser degree, less often, and in fewer circumstances). Moreover, someone who scores a 5 or 6 on the scale would still report and recall different experiences of shyness—and might even self-identify as a "shy person."

WHAT'S IN A NAME?

Yet another reason why shyness is hard to define is because the word *shyness* entered into common usage in the English language long before this phenomenon became of interest to developmental psychologists. The linguistic origins (etymology) of the word *shy* can be traced back to the Middle English word *schey*, which itself was derived from the Old English word *sceoh*. Going back even further, we can trace a Germanic origin to the Old High German word *sciuhen* and Proto-Germanic *skeukh(w)az*.

According to the *Oxford English Dictionary*, the earliest recorded use of the word *shy* (with an intended meaning "easily frightened" [Simpson & Weiner, 1989, p. 401]) is from an Anglo-Saxon poem in about 1000 A.D. By the 1600s, the accepted definition of *shyness* was "to recoil" (*Online Etymology Dictionary*). In 1795, Samuel Johnson's *English Dictionary of Language* provided the concise but descriptive modern definition of *shy* as "reserved, cautious, suspicious" (p. 198)

The word *shyness* is now certainly part of our vernacular for describing children of all ages (as well as adults). Part of its fuzziness can be attributed to the many related terms that have been used as synonyms or to describe related characteristics. We have provided a partial list in Box 1.1. A quick perusal of this list reveals a wide range of terms that relate to many different aspects of shyness. For example, some expressions focus more on emotions related to shyness (e.g., embarrassed, fearful), whereas others pertain to behaviors (e.g., quiet, socially withdrawn). Some evoke more positive connotations (e.g., humble, coy) and others seem more negative (e.g., loner, reclusive). We will argue later that several of these terms should actually not be used interchangeably with shyness, as they refer to quite different phenomena (e.g., introverted, socially anxious).

BOX 1.1. SHYNESS BY ANY OTHER NAME—SYNONYMS FOR SHY

abashed	humble	reserved	socially anxious
bashful	inhibited	reticent	socially withdrawn
circumspect	introverted	retiring	solitary
coy	loner	self-conscious	taciturn
demure	meek	self-effacing	timid
diffident	modest	sensitive	unsociable
embarrassed	mousy	sheepish	wallflower
fearful	quiet	skittish	wary

A BRIEF HISTORY OF SHYNESS

The scientific study of shyness has a rich history. Indeed, many of the central ideas that helped to inform psychologists' conceptualizations and understanding of shyness can be traced back a very long time. For example, over 2,000 years ago, Greek physicians Hippocrates and Galen suggested that we are born with differences in our character that substantially contribute to our patterns of mood (including fear) and social behaviors (including the tendency to be sociable) (for a more detailed description, see Kagan, 1994). In the 1800s, Charles Darwin described characteristics of shyness in animals and humans (and was particularly interested in blushing). Darwin also noted the influence of social context of shy individuals' behaviors, writing in 1872 that "persons who are exceedingly shy are rarely shy in the presence of those with whom they are quite familiar" (Darwin, 1872, p. 330).

One of the first formal descriptions of shyness in the psychological literature was published in 1896 (in the *British Medical Journal*) by physician Harry Campbell. In his essay titled "Morbid Shyness," Campbell described many aspects of shyness that would go on to become central components of subsequent psychological research. For example, Campbell postulated about the origins of shyness in childhood and its developmental course ("A minor degree of shyness, especially in the early years of life, is of course normal"; "shyness is most pronounced at puberty," p. 805), situations that elicit shyness ("shy amongst strangers," "shy of praise," "shyness is so readily induced in a person by his being looked at," p. 806), and common symptoms of how shyness is manifested ("blushing," "cardiac disturbances," "perspiration, especially of the hands," "silence," "inability to look one straight in the face," pp. 806–807).

Almost 30 years later, in a paper published in the *Journal of Neurology and Psychopathology* in 1927, F. A. Hampton suggested that we may regard the shy person in general as suffering from a "conflict between an urge to reach upwards to the normal level from a position of imagined inferiority and a deterrent fear of failure" (p. 126). As we will discuss shortly, the notion that shy children experience a conflict in their motivations to approach and avoid social situations is a key component of the contemporary conceptualization of shyness.

The earliest studies pertaining to shy children at school (that we could find) were conducted in the early 1920s. In 1921, E. L. Richards reported the results of a research study of 18 so-called "backward" and "difficult" 1st-grade children, who were placed in a "special class under a special teacher" and provided with "appropriate treatment and discipline." Richards noted that "marked improvements" in children's social and intellectual functioning were found 1 year later. In interpreting the results, Richards asserted that factors such as shyness may "obscure the native capacity" of a child to the extent that she or he will substantially underperform at school (p. 707, article's abstract). In 1923, C. E. Dealey reported the detailed case histories of 38 "problem children" (p. 125) in kindergarten, grade 1, and grade 2. About half of these children were characterized by "extreme sensitivity or timidity" (p. 135).

So, even in the early 1920s there appeared to be some awareness that shyness could potentially pose a problem for children in educational settings. However, as noted earlier, much more attention was being devoted to disruptive children. This was confirmed by an early study of teachers' beliefs described by E. K. Wickman (1928) in his book *Children's Behavior and Teachers' Attitudes*. Wickman examined teachers' attitudes, beliefs, and responses to a wide range of children's misbehaviors. He concluded that the most serious concerns in the minds of teachers were offenses against property, sex, and truth. Next came misbehaviors that interfered with the successful performance of scholastic work. Finally, behaviors representing social withdrawal (which included shyness and sensitivity) were deemed the least serious.

In 1938, researchers Pearl Lowenstein and Margaret Svendsen reported the results of one of the first intervention programs specifically designed to assist shy children. In a study entitled "Experimental Modification of the Behavior of a Selected Group of Shy and Withdrawn Children," 13 boys aged 6–8 years were initially identified as shy or withdrawn. The entire group was then sent to a small farm camp where, under adult supervision and care, they were essentially left to play with one another over a period of 8 weeks. No other children were present, so the initially shy and withdrawn children had only one another as playmates. According to the researchers, after the completion of this play therapy, follow-up assessments demonstrated improvement in 10 of the 13 children. The researchers concluded that "considerable modification of the behavior of shy children can be affected" (p. 652).

These earliest theories and research studies were remarkably insightful. Indeed, in many ways, these writings laid the foundations for many of our core contemporary ideas about the psychology of children's shyness.

Unfortunately, these early studies were also few and far between. Indeed, shy children were largely ignored in the psychological literature for much of the 20th century. This lack of attention can be attributed to several factors. First, Sigmund Freud's psychoanalytic theory, which predominated for much of this time period, posited that younger children could not really experience true feelings of depression and anxiety until their *superego* (the part of the psyche that tells us to "do what is right") developed when they were older (see Freud, 1964). Second, influential child psychologists like Jean Piaget were much more concerned with children's thinking than their social behaviors. Indeed, in 1959 Piaget (in)famously wrote that "there is, as we have said, no real social life between children of less than 7 or 8 years" (Piaget, 1959, p. 40). As any primary teacher will know all too well, there is an extremely active social life in the kindergarten classroom!

Third, clinical psychologists continually downplayed the importance of childhood shyness as a predictor of later difficulties. For example, in 1954, researcher Don Morris and colleagues (Morris, Soroker, & Buruss, 1954) tracked down and assessed a group of 54 adults who had been previously admitted to a child guidance clinic as shy or withdrawn when they were children. Among their conclusions, they stated that these adults were "on the whole getting along quite well," "one has the impression that most . . . turn out to be average, normal people in most respects," and that we are quite likely "overconcerned about these personality characteristics" (p. 753).

Subsequent reviews and syntheses of the pertinent psychological literature conducted by Lee Robins (1966) and Lawrence Kohlberg (Kohlberg, LaCrosse, & Ricks, 1972) determined that shyness (and related characteristics) were relatively unstable and not really predictive of later difficulties in adolescence and adulthood. However, a closer look at the details of these studies offers some potential retrospective insight into these conclusions. The adolescent and adult outcomes that were found to be largely unrelated to childhood shyness included such things as schizophrenia and juvenile delinquency. We would agree that shy children are not at risk for such later difficulties!

Growing out of these early beginnings, the latter part of the 20th century was witness to considerable increased interest in the development and implications of shyness in childhood. In the next section, we present the contemporary psychological conceptualization, definition, and core components of shyness.

CURRENT VIEWS FROM DEVELOPMENTAL PSYCHOLOGY

As we mentioned earlier, shyness is one of those concepts that is often easier to *know it when you see it* rather than formally define. As we have argued previously (Coplan, Ooi, & Nocita, 2015; Coplan & Rubin, 2010), this has also proven to be true to a certain extent for developmental psychologists. To complicate things even more, developmental psychologists also employ other related terms with subtle but sometimes important differences in meanings. Thus, terms such as *behavioral inhibition, anxious solitude, social reticence* (and others!) make for a confusing and complex set of overlapping labels and concepts. To make things worse, most of these terms ultimately end up essentially used interchangeably with the word *shyness*. Finally, to complicate things even further, there are many other psychological terms which are often used interchangeably with shyness—but actually refer to quite different concepts (e.g., introversion, social anxiety)—but more on that later in this chapter. So, it is perhaps no wonder that developmental psychologists have difficulty agreeing upon a standard definition of shyness.

Further complicating matters, shyness is actually quite difficult to measure—particularly in children—because so much about it concerns internal states, like feelings, thoughts, and motivations. Perhaps as a result, developmental psychologists have employed many different methods for assessing shyness. For older children and adolescents, there is a primary reliance on *self-reports*. For these measures, the child him- or herself answers a series of questions (for example, on a 5-point scale) about how often, how much, or to what extent he or she behaves, thinks, feels, or otherwise experiences various aspects of shyness. Another common methodology for older children is to ask children about other children. For example, we might ask each of the children in a given classroom to nominate the three students in their class who: (1) behave the shyest; (2) most frequently blush; and (3) are least likely to talk. We would then tally up the total number of nominations that each child received, across all of the other children in the class, for each of these items, to generate an overall shyness score.

Young children are less reliable about telling us about their internal states (although the use of visual cues, puppets, and other age-appropriate aids can help). With this group, psychologists are more likely to turn to someone who knows the child very well, like a parent or a teacher, to provide ratings of shyness. As well, shyness has also been measured at multiple age periods using direct observations, typically either in a laboratory playroom, the classroom, or in the schoolyard.

Nevertheless, it is worth noting that when psychologists take different measures of a children's shyness from different sources there is typically only a moderate level of agreement. For example, a child rated as *very shy* at school by a teacher may be rated as *outgoing* by a parent. This may be due in part to measurement error (assessments like this are always imperfect to various degrees). However, as we will discuss in several subsequent chapters, parents and teachers may also disagree about whether a given child is shy because they are privy to this child's behaviors in very different (nonoverlapping) contexts.

Thus, it can certainly be said that developmental psychologists do not all agree on what shyness is and how it should be measured. Having said all that, if we take a step back and look a bit more broadly, we would argue that most definitions and conceptualizations of childhood shyness share a set of common central principles. These key components are listed in Box 1.2. Let's take a more detailed look at each.

Box 1.2. Essential Psychological Components of Childhood Shyness

- Shyness is a temperamental trait.
- Shy children tend to be behaviorally restrained, wary, and fearful when encountering new people or entering new situations.
- Shy children are prone to self-consciousness and embarrassment in situations of perceived social evaluations.
- Shyness is characterized by a conflict between children's motivations to approach and avoid others.

Temperamental Trait

Temperamental traits are child characteristics that are biologically based, typically appear early in life, and are relatively stable over time. You can think of temperament as a core building block of children's developing personality. We will talk in more detail about children's temperament in Chapter 2, but as a starting point, children with different temperaments tend to respond quite differently to their environments, particularly when faced with challenging and stressful situations. In the case of shyness, these stress-provoking situations would almost always involve people!

A major focus of temperament research is children's emotional reactivity (e.g., how easily they become upset or excited) and regulation (e.g., how easily they calm down after becoming upset or excited). In the case of shyness, the two primary emotions of initial interest are fear and anxiety. As an aside, although these terms are often used interchangeably, they actually refer to different emotional processes. Fear occurs in the presence of a concrete stimuli (something that is actually there or is happening right now). For example, if you are camping and a bear walks up to your tent, you would likely feel fear! In contrast, anxiety typically occurs in anticipation of something that may or may not happen in the future. For example, you may have trouble sleeping because you are going camping the next week and you are worried that you will encounter a bear. Repeatedly reflecting, analyzing, or ruminating upon a past event is also a common manifestation of anxiety.

Shy children are prone to both fear and anxiety—typically related to social encounters. For example, shy children may experience anxiety the night before their first day of school, fear when they meet their new class-mates for the first time, and then anxiety again that night thinking back upon their stressful experiences during that first day and anticipating events the following day.

Fear of New People and Situations

Two early and influential approaches to the study of temperament high-lighted the context of *novelty* (unfamiliarity) as a particular challenge for shy children. First, in their now classic studies in the 1960s and 1970s, Alexander Thomas and Stella Chess (1977) sought to describe the basic normative dimensions by which infants might respond to the challenges of their environments. Based on extensive observations of infants and young children, they identified several basic dimensions of temperament (which in-cluded traits like approach/withdrawal and activity/passivity) that appeared early in life. Various combinations of these traits were then synthesized to create three broad temperamental types of children which they labeled easy, difficult, and slow to warm up.

For our purposes, we are most interested in the 15% of young children who were designated as *slow to warm up*. These children showed negative responses and tended to withdraw when exposed to new situations, but then tended to adapt and respond more positively over time and with repeated exposure. A key contribution of this research was the general notion that children displayed characteristic styles of behavioral responses to different environments. In terms of shyness, this referred to a behavioral tendency to be slow in adapting to new situations.

Jerome Kagan and his colleagues (e.g., Kagan, Reznick, Clarke, Snid-man, & Garcia Coll, 1984; Kagan, Reznick, & Snidman, 1987, 1988) brought increased attention to the study of shyness in the early 1980s with their extensive studies of a temperamental trait that Kagan labeled *behav-ioral inhibition*. He observed young children's responses to a series of un-familiar events, including meeting an adult stranger, encountering a set of new toys, exposure to a large and odd-looking robot, and being separated from their mothers. Kagan found that about 15% of children could be characterized as extremely *inhibited*, reacting to novelty with a consistent pattern of wariness, hesitancy, and reserve. Typical behaviors of inhibit-ed children when encountering something new included crying, clinging to mother, long latencies (delays) to speak, and withdrawal. Among the many influential findings of Kagan's extensive research was that behavior-al inhibition was among the most stable temperamental traits across the lifespan. As well, Kagan emphasized the biological bases of behavioral inhibition—arguing that inhibited children evidenced unique patterns of reactivity in their central nervous systems when faced with stressful situa-tions (see Chapter 2).

Self-Consciousness When Perceiving Evaluation

Also in the 1980s, temperament researcher Arnold Buss (1986) proposed that there are two distinct types of shyness. The first is called *fearful* shyness; Buss argued that this is a heritable trait that emerges during the latter part of the first year of life. Fearful shyness is basically described as fear/wariness of strangers, a concept quite similar to Kagan's behavioral inhibition. However, in the case of fear shyness, there is a narrower focus on novel *social* situations (i.e., involving people) as compared to the broader focus of behavioral inhibition as fear of novelty in general.

The second type of shyness is called *self-conscious* shyness. Self-conscious shyness is thought to be later appearing (emerging at age 4 to 5 years) and argued to be more influenced by children's experiences. Rather than involving fear, this type of shyness is believed to reflect the tendency to experience feelings of self-consciousness and embarrassment in situations of perceived social evaluation (e.g., being the center of attention). Buss originally argued that fearful shyness and self-conscious shyness were largely distinct constructs. However, subsequent research suggests that these different types of shyness share considerable overlap, with older children often displaying signs of both.

From a developmental perspective, the emergence of self-conscious shyness coincides with the maturation of children's social-cognitive system, particularly the abilities to take on others' perspectives. Toddlers and young preschoolers have difficulty understanding that other people see the world differently from themselves. This phenomenon is called *egocentrism* (or literally "it's all about me!"). For example, if a toddler likes to eat pickles with ice cream, she will simply assume that everyone else must like that too. However, by age 4 to 5 years, children start to come to realize that other people often have very different thoughts, opinions, and likes/dislikes than they do. This ongoing maturation of social-cognitive abilities brings children to the understanding that others may view them differently than they view themselves—which in turn allows children to contemplate how others view them (e.g., see themselves through the eyes of others).

Although this is a normal developmental progression for all children, for shy children this *public self-awareness* more often leads to concerns about self-presentation (how do I appear to others?) and social evaluation (how am I being appraised by others?). As a result, situations where a child perceives him/herself as being the center of attention or as being evaluated by others trigger heightened feelings of self-consciousness and embarrassment.

At school, such situations are exceedingly common! From the earliest session of show-and-tell, to getting called on in class, to oral presentations, children at school are constantly placed in situations where they are actually being formally appraised and evaluated by others. Moreover, shyness is also evoked in situations where children simply *perceive* themselves as being evaluated. For shy children, such situations may include working in a group with other children and having to talk to a teacher, principal, or other person in a position of authority.

Indeed, shy children are prone to feel as though others are evaluating them pretty much any time attention is drawn to them. A few years ago in a workshop with parents, a mother asked for help because her 4-year-old shy child was being "disrespectful and disobedient." When asked to elaborate, she told a story from her child's last birthday party. The child received a very nice present from her grandmother. Everyone oohed and aahed after the child opened the present, and then the mother asked the child to say thank you to her grandmother. This led to an anticipatory silence in the audience as everyone's eyes turned to the child. The child buried her head in her arms and, despite repeated requests from her mother, refused to speak. This mother reported being extremely frustrated, disappointed, and embarrassed that her child would not simply say thank you (see Chapter 3 for a detailed discussion about parental responses to children's shy behaviors). However, for this shy child, just having the eyes of friends and family upon her was enough to create substantial stress that caused her to freeze.

In fact, some shy children may become embarrassed and feel highly self-conscious even when they receive positive attention. For example, a teacher who praises a shy child in front of the class for a correctly spoken answer may actually be reducing the likelihood of that child speaking up again in the future. Instead, a private whispered aside ("by the way, your answer before was great!") later during a quiet moment will have the desired effect of positive reinforcement without the accompanying discomfort of being publicly singled out (see Chapter 8 for more on specific strategies for teachers to help shy children).

Approach-Avoidance Conflict

In the early 1990s, Jens Asendorpf (1990) proposed the idea that there are different types of socially withdrawn and sociable children. His idea was based on different combinations of children's motivations to approach and to avoid social situations. For example, *sociable* children were characterized as highly motivated to seek the rewards of social interactions (high social-approach motivation) and at the same time, they derive considerable pleasure and feel very comfortable when participating in these social encounters (low social-avoidance motivations).

As we saw in some of the early writings about shyness, it has long been suggested that shy individuals experience a tug-of-war of conflicting feelings and thoughts. According to Asendorpf's model, shyness is a reflection of an underlying struggle between children's social-approach and social-avoidance motivations. That is, shy children experience an *approach-avoidance* conflict, an internal battle between their desire for social interaction with peers (high social-approach motivation) and the stresses that are simultaneously evoked by these same social interactions (high social-avoidance motivations). Simply stated, shy children often want to play with others but these inclinations are subdued by accompanying fears and anxieties.

This internal struggle can often be observed in shy children in the schoolyard, playground, or other informal social situations. For example, a shy child will often look over and appear interested in a group of other children playing. The child will then slowly start to approach this group, inching closer until he is just at the edge of the social sphere. At this point, the child's advance will stall, and he will be left hovering nearby, watching the other children, but making no attempts to join in. After some time, the shy child might eventually start to play alone, but near the others.

As we mentioned earlier, children may retreat to solitude for many different reasons. For example, as we have learned so far, shy children tend to spend more time in solitude because, despite a desire to engage with others, social exchanges are stressful for them. Asendorpf's (1990) model is particularly useful for differentiating shyness from another subtype of social withdrawal that he labeled *unsociability* (sometimes called *social disinterest*). According to the model, unsociable children are not particularly motivated to play with other children (low social-approach motivation). But at the same time, they will not go out of their way to refuse an attractive social invitation (low social-avoidance motivation). Thus, unsociability can be construed as a nonfearful preference for solitary activities.

As an example, an unsociable child at school would be content to spend free time reading a book, drawing a picture, or doing a puzzle alone. If a group of children invited this child to join them in a fun-looking board game, the unsociable child will likely join them for a while, and then return to playing alone at the completion of the game. Research indicates that unsociable children generally get along quite well at school and are not at increased risk for social and emotional difficulties. In this regard, unsociability is considered to be a comparatively *benign* form of social withdrawal.

However, shy and unsociable children can sometimes be difficult to differentiate in the school context. For example, both shy and unsociable children might be observed to be off by themselves outside during recess. Similarly, both shy and unsociable children may not be overly talkative during group-oriented activities in class. Notwithstanding, important differences between the two children would likely be occurring *internally*. In the case of the unsociable child, there could be quiet contentment and satisfaction in being engaged in a solitary but productive endeavor. In contrast, the shy child may be feeling stressed, lonely, and upset that he is not able to join his peers in play.

WHAT SHYNESS IS *NOT*

After spending much of this chapter describing what shyness *is*, we will end with a brief discussion of what shyness *is not*. As we saw in the list provided previously, there are lots of terms used as synonyms for shyness in common language. We have also seen that psychologists use a number of different terms to describe constructs that share a fair amount of overlap with how we have defined shyness herein (e.g., behavioral inhibition, slow to warm up, fearful shyness, self-conscious shyness). However, there are two particular terms present in both the vernacular and in the psychological literature that are often used interchangeably with shyness—but (at least to us) are clearly *not* shyness. We think it is particularly important for teachers to understand these distinctions.

First, we would like to distinguish between shyness and *introversion*. Introversion-Extroversion is one of the Big Five traits that are thought to comprise the basic dimensions of personality. The other Big Five traits are agreeableness, neuroticism/emotional stability, openness to experience, and conscientiousness. *Introversion* is a broad concept that has been a central focus of personality researchers dating back to Hans Eysenck in the 1940s (Eysenck, 1947). It has also been the recipient of considerable attention in the media and popular press (e.g., Cain, 2012).

A simple definition of an *introvert* is someone whose motives and actions are turned inward, and who is energized by spending time alone. For introverts, being in a crowd of people is overstimulating and draining, and they will seek a retreat into solitude to recharge their batteries. By way of contrast, extroverts are energized by social situations and find it more difficult to tolerate being alone (where they are understimulated). Of note, although introverts are often also described as shy, being among people is not necessarily anxiety-provoking for them, it is just tiring. Thus, although some introverts may indeed be shy (particularly if they are also high in the trait of neuroticism), others are not, and would be better described as unsociable.

Finally, we would like to distinguish between shyness and Social Anxiety Disorder (SAD). Social Anxiety Disorder is defined by the American Psychiatric Association (2013) as a debilitating mental health disorder characterized by an intense and persistent fear/anxiety of one or more social situations in which a person is exposed to unfamiliar people or possible scrutiny by others. SAD (previously known as Social Phobia) is the most common type of anxiety disorder, estimated to affect close to one out of every eight individuals during their lifetimes.

There is certainly a degree of underlying conceptual similarity between shyness and SAD. Indeed, some psychologists would argue that the difference is really one of *degree*. That is, people with SAD are just really, really, really shy. However, even among extremely shy children, the majority do not go on to develop SAD. Moreover, some individuals develop SAD without having grown up as shy (we discuss the importance of this distinction in more detail in Chapter 4).

REVIEW OF KEY TERMS RELATED TO CHILDHOOD SHYNESS

- *Approach-Avoidance Conflict:* Internal conflict between the desire for social interaction (social-approach motivation) and the simultaneous fear/anxiety of social interactions (social-avoidance motivation)
- *Behavioral Inhibition:* Biologically based tendency to react to meeting new people and encountering new events with a consistent pattern of wariness, hesitancy, and reserve
- *Fearful Shyness:* Early-appearing and heritable type of shyness related to fear/wariness of strangers
- *Introversion:* A personality trait characterized by an inner focus and the tendency to be energized by time spent alone
- *Self-Conscious Shyness:* Late-appearing and environment-influenced type of shyness related to self-consciousness/embarrassment of being the center of attention
- *Slow-to-Warm-Up Child:* Young child who displays negative responses and withdraws when exposed to new situations, but tends to adapt and respond more positively over time and with repeated exposure
- *Social-Anxiety Disorder:* A debilitating mental health disorder characterized by an intense and persistent fear/anxiety of one or more social situations in which a person is exposed to unfamiliar people or possible scrutiny by others
- *Social Withdrawal:* Process whereby children remove themselves from available opportunities for social interaction (e.g., playing along in the presence of peers)
- *Temperament:* Biologically based, early appearing, and stable individual differences in children's emotional and behavioral patterns and responses
- *Unsociability:* A nonfearful preference for solitary activities

CHAPTER 2

The Nature of Shyness
Genetics and Biological Foundations

FIVE QUIRKY FACTS ABOUT SHYNESS

1. Shy infants are more often conceived just before the winter months.

2. Shy adults have a better sense of smell than non-shy adults.

3. Shy children and their families are more likely to suffer from hay fever and other allergies.

4. Shy children have warmer finger tips on their left hand than on their right hand.

5. Shy children are more likely to have blue eyes.

Sigmund Freud once claimed that "anatomy is destiny" (1924, p. 178). Could this be true in terms of shyness? Is it possible that some children are just *born* shy? The answer to this provocative question has profound implications for everything from our basic understanding of how shyness develops, to our expectations about how shy children might change, to the strategies we might employ to assist shy children who are struggling at school. In this chapter we attempt to tackle this complex issue and consider the biological foundations of childhood shyness.

Many pet owners would probably agree that dogs can differ in terms of shyness and boldness. In fact, differences in shyness have been studied and demonstrated in a wide range of nonhuman species. For example, Stephen Suomi (1991) has conducted a series of studies examining differences in the shy behaviors and responses of rhesus monkeys. From birth, the majority of monkeys adapt well to challenges and new situations, are quick to explore, and do not tend to get upset easily. Suomi calls these types of monkeys *laid back*. In contrast, about 20% of rhesus monkeys are born with the tendency to be fearful, vigilant, and cautious when they are faced with new situations and other challenges. Does this sound familiar? This description bears striking resemblance to the extremely inhibited children that Jerome Kagan and colleagues (Kagan et al., 1984) first studied (as described in Chapter

1). Suomi calls this subgroup *uptight* monkeys. Several other researchers have demonstrated similar differences in shyness across many other species, including horses, goats, pigs, birds, lizards, and even fish and octopi! Such differences strongly suggest the influence of biology.

We begin Chapter 2 by discussing the heritability of shyness. Does shyness run in families? If so, can we attribute any of this to genetics? We then shift the focus of the chapter to a more detailed discussion of the biological foundations of shyness. This will include an overview of what happens inside our bodies when we get scared. As it turns out, some of the ways that our brains and bodies respond to fear appear to be involved when shy children encounter a stressful social situation, like meeting a new person. The main premise we will highlight is that shy children may be *wired* somewhat differently from their more bold classmates. We will consider what implications this might have for how shy children feel, think, and behave. Finally, interspersed throughout this chapter, we will revisit and try to explain the various *quirky facts* about shyness that were listed at the outset of this chapter. Some of these effects remain unexplained (take a second to guess which ones—you may be surprised later!).

BORN SHY? HEREDITY AND THE ROLE OF GENETICS

> No fact is more certain than that shyness runs in families. (Harry Campbell, 1896, p. 805)

As evidenced by this quote, we have apparently known about the heritability of shyness for quite some time. There have been many studies showing that extremely shy or anxious children are generally more likely to grow up in homes with shy or anxious parents (for a recent review see Negreiros & Miller, 2014). However, it is difficult to draw conclusions from these studies as to exactly why this is the case. One of the main reasons is because such similarities in shyness between parents and children can be due to both *nature* (e.g., parents may pass on genes related to shyness to their children) and *nurture* (shy parents may engage in child-rearing behaviors that foster shyness in their children).

The nature versus nurture question has been one of the most central and hotly contested debates in the history of developmental psychology. Are we the products of our genes, our environment, or some combination of both? In the 17th and 18th centuries, philosophers fiercely deliberated the answer to the basic question of *nature or nurture*. Several prominent thinkers were firmly on the side of nature. For example, in his doctrine of original sin, Thomas Hobbes (1909/1651) suggested that children were born inherently selfish and with a tendency toward evil. It was thus up to parents and society to shepherd them into goodness. Jean-Jacques Rousseau (1984/1755) also believed that children had innate characteristics and tendencies. However, according to his doctrine of innate purity, children came into the world as *noble savages*, with an intuitive sense of right and wrong that predisposed them to being good. It was society that later served to tempt them toward misbehavior and sin. In contrast, other approaches solely favored the influence of nurture. For example, John Locke (1823/1689) postulated that children were born as a *tabula rasa* (blank slate). From this perspective, children's characteristics and behaviors were completely determined by the influence of the environment, based on their upbringing and other experiences. Thus, should the children turn out badly or behave in ways misaligned with expectations of the time, it was surely the fault of the parents!

With the emergence of the contemporary science of genetics it became clear that this initial question of *which one*, nature *or* nurture, was not adequate. Our increased knowledge about how traits are passed on to offspring was accompanied by a better understanding of how environmental factors also play a role. This evolved into the research approach called *behavioral genetics*, which attempts to answer the question: *how much of each*? (or nature *and* nurture). Behavioral genetics studies are deigned to estimate the *heritability* of different traits by comparing similarities and differences in the characteristics of individuals sharing genetic material at varying percentages, such as twins, siblings, and parents with children.

The underlying rationale for these types of studies is derived from the various possible genetic compositions of different types of siblings. For example, identical twins (also called monozygotic) are conceived from a single fertilized ovum and thus share 100% of the same genetic materials. In contrast, fraternal twins (also called dizygotic) are conceived from two separate ova, each fertilized by a separate sperm. As a result, just like non-twin siblings, fraternal twins share about 50% of their genes. If we assume that all children in a family are raised in roughly the same environment (this is actually not a simple assumption—but more on this later), then if identical twins are more alike on a given trait than fraternal twins, the reason for this increased similarity can be attributed to the influence of shared genes (i.e., nature), rather than the ways they were parented, the culture in which they were living, or other environmental effects (i.e., nurture).

There have been numerous studies where this has been attempted with children's shyness. Results vary depending upon how shyness is assessed and at what age twins were compared. For example, in one twin study, researcher Hill Goldsmith and colleagues (Goldsmith, Lemery, Buss, & Campos, 1999) calculated that observed fear of strangers in infancy was 68% heritable. In another twin study with older children and adolescents, Sheila McGuire and colleagues (McGuire, Clifford, Fink, Basho, & McDonnell, 2003) reported that shy behaviors with adults were 51% heritable.

Overall, identical twins are generally found to be much more similar than fraternal twins in terms of shyness (particularly in infancy and toddlerhood). Indeed, across studies, shyness typically demonstrates moderate to high levels of heritability, with some findings suggesting that over 70% of the variability in young children's shyness can be attributed to genetic factors (see Clifford, Lemery-Chalfant, & Goldsmith, 2015).

However, there are reasons to be cautious in how we interpret the implications of this type of research. To begin with, the core assumption that all children in the same family (even pairs of identical twins) grow up experiencing the same environment turns out to be overly simplistic and flawed. For example, not only do parents tend to treat their different children differently, but different children can respond quite differently to the same environmental event. Imagine a situation where twins hear their parents arguing—while the first sibling goes to hide in his room, the second one runs downstairs and yells at his parents to stop fighting.

Moreover, it is virtually impossible to fully separate genetic and environmental influences. For example, as we will see in the next chapter, children who are born shy not only evoke different responses from different parents, but also respond very differently than non-shy children to specific patterns of parenting behaviors. And, of course, children are not passive recipients of their environments. They actively shape and interpret their own experiences through their choices and behaviors. A shy adolescent who elects to become a computer programmer will experience a very different social environment than a sociable adolescent who pursues a career in sales. Thus, contemporary views not only acknowledge the contributions of both nature and nurture to development, but also consider the complex interplay among these influences.

In recent years, researchers have also begun to look at genetic effects related to shyness (and many other traits) more directly at the molecular level (e.g., Battaglia et al., 2005; Rubin et al., 2013; Smith et al., 2012). Advances in technology now allow for relatively easy and nonintrusive collection (e.g., using saliva) and analysis of genetic materials. In these molecular genetic studies, researchers have examined variations in specific genes that are theorized to be related to shyness. There may be potential in this approach, but findings to date have been somewhat inconsistent. Continuing advances in methods may improve the results. For example, like most other complex traits, there is little chance that a single gene is responsible for the characteristic of shyness. It is much more likely that several different genes interact and combine to influence the complex set of behaviors, emotions, and thought patterns that encompass shyness. We have really only begun to scratch the surface in terms of uncovering how this might work.

Moreover, even interpreting the results of these direct molecular genetic studies remains challenging. As we have already seen, genetic predispositions (i.e., nature) interact with and influence the environment over time (e.g., children respond differently to the same environmental event, children with different characteristics seek out different environments). However, recent theory and research suggest that the environment can also switch genes on and off and directly alter DNA (this idea is called *epigenetics*). Thus, the environment appears to be able to directly influence genetics!

So where does this leave us? Shyness is a temperamental trait. As we described in Chapter 1, temperamental traits are believed to have biological bases and appear very early in life. So far in this chapter evidence has suggested that part of these *nature*-based predispositions do come from genetics. In short, there is reason to believe that shyness does run in families, at least to a certain degree. But, shyness is certainly not the result of genetics alone: It is much more complex than that! Moreover, it is also important to note that *nature* effects are not solely based on genetics. Our biological characteristics can be affected by prenatal and neonatal stresses, the utero environment, a difficult birth, and many other factors.

As an example of this, let's revisit our first *quirky fact* about shyness listed at the outset of the chapter. As you may recall, it was that shy children are more likely to be conceived just before the winter months. This tidbit of information comes from a study by researcher Stephen Gortmaker (Gortmaker, Kagan, Caspi, & Shiva, 1997), who examined the link between mothers' exposure to natural sunlight during pregnancy and children's shyness after birth. Using samples from the United States and New Zealand (to show the effect in both the Northern and Southern Hemispheres), Gortmaker found that children of mothers whose second trimester occurred during winter months (where there is the least natural sunlight) were more shy than children whose mothers were exposed to greater amounts of sunlight. The effect was not huge—there was only about a 20% greater likelihood of being shy when the second trimester occurred during winter—and the mechanism explaining this association is not well understood. However, this finding does illustrate that when we consider whether some children are born shy, we need to include a wide range of factors and processes that may influence our biological makeup. In the case of shy children, the type of biological processes that appear to be more relevant have to do with responses to fear. Thus, in the next section, we provide a brief overview of what researchers have found to happen inside our bodies when we get scared.

THE FEAR SYSTEM: THE ANATOMY OF FIGHT VERSUS FLIGHT

We all know the physical signs of fear. When we feel scared, our heart races, our palms sweat, we breathe quickly, our muscles tense, and our pupils widen. Why does this happen? What is going on inside our brain and body that is causing these symptoms? Researchers have actually learned quite a bit about the fear system and how it works. Of course, this book is not the venue for a detailed description of the physiological and neurological processes that underlie our perceptions and reactions to fear. However, for shy children, social situations (like meeting a new person) may trigger just this type of response.

Imagine you are walking in a secluded forest by yourself. It is starting to get dark, you have wandered off the beaten path, and you are not exactly sure where you are. There are lots of unidentified noises, scuttling movements in the periphery of your vision, and even some strange smells. Your senses are on high alert, rapidly scanning the area on the lookout for signs of danger. Suddenly, in front of you, a large bear steps onto the path. What happens next inside you occurs so quickly that you are not consciously aware of it. In the blink of an eye, your brain and body swing into action to automatically prepare you to deal with this potential threat to your safety. First, your senses register the bear as a possible source of danger. This information is immediately sent to an area of your brain called the *amygdala*, which is involved in the processing of fear and other emotions. The role of the amygdala is to decode and interpret the information inputted through the senses. If a threat is perceived, it then acts like an alarm and sends a distress signal to another part of the brain called the *hypothalamus*. The hypothalamus functions as the communication and command center. It uses the nervous system to quickly send instructions to various other parts of the body about how to respond to this threat.

When we are faced with danger, our most basic options are either *fight* or *flight*. Our rapid response system to threat evolved to protect us in times of imminent danger. In response to the call to action issued by the hypothalamus, a series of physiological reactions is triggered. For example, the adrenal gland is activated, increasing the production of hormones pumped into the bloodstream, including epinephrine (also known as adrenaline) and cortisol (also known as the stress hormone). The job of these hormones is to prepare the body to either defend itself or to flee. This is done by increasing heart rate and blood pressure (so blood flows more efficiently to the heart and other vital organs), making us breathe more rapidly (so our lungs can take in more oxygen and send it to places where it is most needed), and tensing up our muscles (so we are primed to react).

All of this happens so quickly that we may not even be aware of these changes until after they have occurred. Have you ever experienced a near miss, such that you *almost* had a major accident? Remember how you felt immediately after you realized everything was okay? It is likely that your heart was beating rapidly, and you may have felt a little light-headed. These are the symptoms of the fight-or-flight response.

Jerome Kagan was among the first researchers to connect our knowledge of the fear system to shy children. As you may recall from Chapter 1, Kagan (Kagan et al., 1984) identified a group of about 15% of children who responded to new situations and unfamiliar people with significant wariness and fear (he called these children extremely *inhibited*). He noticed that some of the behaviors that shy children demonstrated when encountering a threat (like meeting a stranger or encountering a new situation) appeared to be similar to fear-based responses observed in animals—both displayed "freezing" behavior (momentary inability to move in the face of fear). Kagan speculated that such behaviors could be the result of an overactive amygdala. Recall that the amygdala is responsible for sounding the alarm in the face of perceived threat. If extremely shy children have an amygdala that is very easily triggered, then there should be more evidence of the physiological changes that accompany this alarm among shy children.

Results from several subsequent studies have revealed exactly that. In stressful social situations, shy and non-shy children tend to differ in their physiological responses. For example, as compared to their more outgoing peers, shy children have higher heart rates, greater muscle tension, and higher levels of the stress hormone cortisol (e.g., Fox, Henderson, Marshall, Nichols, & Ghera, 2005; Pérez-Edgar, Schmidt, Henderson, Schulkin, & Fox, 2008; Schmidt et al., 1997). All of these physiological responses are consistent with what happens when the amygdala sends out a distress call to the rest of the body to prepare for fight or flight. Subsequent research with adults using more advanced imaging technologies (like fMRI) has measured activity in the amygdala directly in shy and non-shy individuals (e.g., Beaton et al., 2008). The results confirmed what Kagan hypothesized. In response to a perceived social threat (like meeting a stranger), shy children's fear systems are more easily activated and induce greater physiological changes.

With this in mind, let's revisit our second *quirky fact* about shyness, which indicated that shy people may have a more sensitive sense of smell (e.g., Herbener, Kagan, & Cohen, 1989). As we just saw, part of what happens inside us when we get scared is that our senses become more attuned to detect threats. This can result in heightened sensory sensitivity. If shy individuals have a nervous system that is wired to be hypervigilant to social dangers, this may have the side effect of making *all* senses more sensitive. Thus, olfactory senses would be more sensitive to small changes in odor.

THE TIGHTLY COILED SPRING

It was perhaps not surprising to find that shy children's fear system is more reactive to social threats. However, it turns out there is more to this story. There is growing research suggesting that shy children demonstrate these physioliogical differences even at *baseline*. That is, even when they are not immediately under threat, shy children's physiological characteristics such as heart rate and cortisol are higher than those of their less shy counterparts.

For example, research by Louis Schmidt and colleagues (Schmidt, Fox, Rubin, Sternberg, Gold, Smith, et al., 1997) showed that extremely shy children had higher levels of cortisol than non-shy children when it was measured first thing in the morning (when cortisol is typically at its lowest level). Jerome Kagan's (Kagan et al., 1987, 1988) work with shy children actually began when they were in infancy, and his work showed that 4-month-old infants who later became shy children were very easily aroused and upset when shown a colorful mobile. On the other hand, infants who later became bold children were not easily aroused, and maintained a relaxed and calm demeanor when shown the mobile. This suggests that the fear and arousal system of shy children may be somewhat more primed for danger even when there is no immediate danger present.

This brings us back to the third *quirky shyness* fact. Research by Kagan (Kagan et al., 1984) found elevated levels of hay fever and other allergies among shy children and their family members. The mechanism for how this works is not well understood. However, it has been speculated that some of the physiological processes associated with shyness may place increased stress on immune system functioning. For example, heightened cortisol levels over time can weaken the body's ability to fight off sickness. Consistent with this idea, Joanna Chung and Mary Ann Evans (2000) found that shy children were more likely to report symptoms of illness than non-shy children over the course of a 4-week period.

When we talk to parents about the biology of shyness, we do not typically go into this level of detail regarding parts of the brain, the central nervous system, or levels of stress hormones. Instead, we offer the metaphor that many shy children have a nervous system that seems to be wired like a *tightly coiled spring* that is easily set off by social stressors. It is almost as if shy children's bodies are constantly trying to warn them that something scary is about to jump out from around the corner at any time! As a parent once said to us about her shy child, "she tends to feel . . . *everything.*" It is no wonder that shy children have such an intense and visceral response to stressful social situations.

With this in mind, let's revisit the bear in the woods fear scenario, but this time using an example of a shy child coming to meet his teacher on the first day of school. As the child enters the schoolyard, his eyes (and other senses) are rapidly scanning for signs of danger (e.g., other children, teachers, other people in authority). When he sees the teacher, he registers a potential threat (in this case, an unfamiliar adult in a position of authority). His amygdala sets off the alarm and the fear system is activated. So by the time the teacher approaches him to say hello, his body is already primed to run away. It is easy to see how these automatic physiological processes might promote associated shy thoughts, feelings, and behaviors. Indeed, imagine how hard it would be not to feel and act scared when your heart is racing, your breathing is rapid, and cortisol is flooding into your system.

There are certainly potential implications here. Recall Freud's (1924) claim that "anatomy is destiny" (p. 178). This suggests that biological predispositions are going to be difficult to change. Indeed, shy children may always initially have a fearlike response inside when meeting a new person. But that does not mean that shy children cannot learn and develop strategies that will enable them to cope with these initial reactions and move on in an adaptive way. As we will see in the next and subsequent chapters, shy children's experiences in the family and at school are extremely influential contributors to their social, emotional, and academic well-being. Thus, despite Freud's claim, our genes and biology do not define us. Indeed, Freud's quote is more often recast these days as biology is *not* destiny.

Having said that, the biological components of shyness (and other temperamental traits), underscore the idea that children are *predisposed* to respond to the world in different ways. We need to respect these differences and understand that they have wide-ranging implications for how children think, feel, and behave, and that this varies depending on the context (such as home or school). As we will see in later chapters, this is also particularly important to keep in mind when parents (and teachers) set expectations for their efforts to change shy children's responses and reactions. As we say to parents, temperamentally shy young children are not very likely to grow up to be super outgoing and extroverted adults. However, there is no reason to believe that they can't grow up to be well-adjusted and happy human beings.

FINGERTIPS AND LITTLE BOY BLUE-EYES

Admittedly, this has been a pretty heavy chapter in terms of content. With that in mind, we would like to finish on a lighter note with some explanation about our last two *quirky shyness* facts (both of which may have sounded like they were made up!). It may come as a surprise that at least one of these phenomena is actually quite well understood.

We'll start with the fact about shy children having warmer fingertips on the left hand than the right hand. Why might this be the case? This appears to be explainable based on other differences in brain responses demonstrated between shy and non-shy children. Researcher Nathan Fox and his colleagues (Fox, Henderson, Rubin, Calkins, & Schmidt, 2001) have shown that when shy children encounter social stressors, their brains respond with a burst of increased activity (energy) in a specific area located in the right frontal lobe. For very sociable and bold children, this increased energy is more likely to be seen in the left frontal lobe. A similar pattern of right frontal lobe imbalance has been demonstrated in adults suffering from anxiety and depression. How is this related to fingertip temperature? Well, the left and right side of our brains connect to our bodies cross-laterally. This essentially means that the right side of the brain controls the left side of the body, and vice versa. As a result, increased energy in one side of the brain results in very small increases in temperature in the other side of the body. So, using very sensitive thermometers, we can measure the increase in right frontal brain activity among shy children as a small increase in temperature in the finger tip of the left-hand index finger.

The last quirky fact is that shy children are more likely to have blue eyes. As crazy as this may sound, it turns to be a well-replicated effect. Picture 100 extremely shy White children placed in a room together, and another 100 outgoing White children in another room nearby. If you then counted the number of blue-eyed and brown-eyed children in each room, what you would most likely find is a higher proportion of blue-eyed children in the shy room than in the non-shy room. It was again Jerome Kagan (Rosenberg & Kagan, 1987) who first brought this to light, but it has since been replicated in several subsequent studies with infants, toddlers, and school-aged children (Reznick, Gibbons, Johnson, & McDonough, 1989; Rosenberg & Kagan, 1989; Rubin & Both, 1989). The effect also seems to be stronger among boys than girls (Coplan, Coleman, & Rubin, 1998). It was first suggested that this might have something to do with ethnic or cultural factors. For example, individuals with Northern European backgrounds may be more likely to have blue eyes and act in a more reserved fashion. In contrast, Southern Europeans are more likely to have brown eyes and be socialized to be more outgoing. However, it turns out that this phenomenon persists even after controlling for ethnic background. Although some neurological and physiological mechanisms have been proposed to account for this association, to date we really do not know why this is the case. However, even though you may have been surprised to learn about this research, you may be more familiar with the link between shyness and eye color than you were aware.

In a fascinating study, Doreen Arcus (1989) examined the link between eye color and shyness in classic Disney cartoon movie characters. Lo and behold, she found that, overall, shy and vulnerable cartoon characters were more likely to have been drawn with blue eyes, whereas dominant and outgoing characters were more likely to be drawn with brown eyes. It seems reasonable to assume that although animators may get instructions about some aspects of the appearance of the characters they draw, details like eye color may be more likely to be left up to them. Accordingly, Arcus suggested that the illustrators of these characters may have been (subconsciously) influenced by their own personal experiences with blue-eyed shy children. Thus, when it came down to drawing the eye colors of these different characters, drawing blue eyes for the shy ones just sort of seemed right, since this was reflective of the illustrators own real-world experiences with such children.

As a final point, although we have provided evidence of links between certain physical and physiological responses and shyness, these associations are by no means absolute. Thus, some shy children may not be wired in the way that we have described, and some children with these highly reactive nervous systems will turn out to be not shy at all. Nature is only one piece of the puzzle when it comes to influences on children's personality. In the next chapter, we shift our attention to nurture, and discuss the role of parents in the development of shyness.

CHAPTER 3

Nurtured to Be Shy
Attachment and Parenting

CASE STUDY: A VISIT TO THE SWIMMING POOL

Once upon a time, there were two parents each trying to teach their children how to swim. Upon arrival at the swimming pool for the first lesson, each of their children said "I am too scared to go in the water!" and started to cry.

The first parent got angry and said, "Too bad! You need to learn how to swim," and then literally threw the child into the pool.

Over at the other side of the pool, the second parent became very worried and said, "It's okay, don't be upset, you don't have to do it," and then simply took the child home.

The moral of this story is that neither of those two children learned how to swim that day.

Teachers interact with the parents of children in their classes on a regular basis. The topic of a student's shyness might come up in informal discussions (e.g., during drop-off) or during more formal contexts (parent-teacher conference)—and concerns arising from a child's shyness might be expressed by the parent or the teacher. In this chapter, we will provide an overview of developmental psychology research related to the influence of parents in the development of childhood shyness.

As we discussed in Chapter 2, there is strong evidence to suggest biological and genetic components of shyness. However, shy children's *family environment* also plays a critical role in their development. Positive relationships with important others are a significant source of resiliency for a wide range of children at risk. Of course, parent-child relationships are a natural starting point to explore in this regard. We will also discuss parental beliefs, emotional reactions, and behaviors that might be particularly helpful, or not so helpful, for shy children. We end the chapter with some advice for teachers for their interactions with the parents of shy children in their classes.

HOW DO I LOVE THEE?
SHYNESS AND ATTACHMENT RELATIONSHIPS

Psychologist Sigmund Freud once wrote that the infant-mother relationship was "unique, without parallel, established unalterably for a whole life-time as the first and strongest love-object and as the prototype for all later love-relations" (1938, p. 188). Like many aspects of Freud's psychoanalytic theory, it would be fair to say that this assertion turned out to be somewhat of an overstatement. However, Freud's legacy in this domain remains intact. It is now widely accepted that the quality of young children's early relationships with parents (and other important people) have substantive and long-term implications for their development.

Attachment theory arose from Freud's ideas and early seminal work by researchers such as John Bowlby (1973) and Mary Ainsworth (Ainsworth, Blehar, Waters, & Wall, 1978). The central thrust of this theory postulates that children's early relationship experiences with primary caregivers foster the development of more generalized beliefs about the self and others, which influence how we interpret events and form expectations about relationships with others. These broader patterns of views and expectations are called *internal working models*. Metaphorically, internal working models can be thought of as the *lenses* through which we view the world.

Let's illustrate with an example. Most children develop what would be labeled a *secure* parent-child relationship. In ambiguous, threatening, or stressful situations, children in secure relationships feel safe and protected by the presence of their parents. They will turn to and be comforted by their parents. Secure children also come to learn they can rely on their parents to comfort them when they are feeling upset. As a result, the parent functions as a *secure base* from which young children can explore and learn about their environment. Secure parent-child attachment relationships are thought to promote children's confidence, independence, agency, and comfort in social situations. Moreover, as they grow, children with secure relationships are expected to develop more positive views about other people and the world they live in. Such a positive internal working model could be broadly summarized as the view that *the world is a predictable and nice place.*

However, some children develop insecure relationships with their primary caregiver(s). Some insecure relationships are characterized by anger and mistrust (typically called *insecure-avoidant*). More relevant for our purposes, another type of insecure attachment is called *insecure-resistant* (or *insecure-ambivalent*). Insecure-resistant children do not feel very protected or safe when they are with their parents in ambiguous or threatening situations. Instead, they tend to get upset, cling to parents, and fail to explore. Moreover, although they may crave comfort and seek it from parents, insecure-resistant children are not easily soothed by parents in situations when they do get upset. This type of insecure attachment is predictive of later behavior problems in children, including internalizing problems such as anxiety. As they grow, children with insecure-resistant relationships tend to develop more negative views and expectations about themselves and others. This particular type of negative internal working model could be summarized overall as *the world is an unpredictable and scary place.* In this case, such children come to view the world through a lens distorted by fear and anxiety.

Attachment relationships are thought to have *emergent* properties. That is, the quality of any specific relationship is not strictly predictable from the characteristics of the individuals involved in the relationship. By way of illustration, think of a time when you might have tried to set up two friends on a blind date. Based on everything you know about your two friends, you had assumed they would be absolutely perfect for each other. However, when they met, things just did not work out at all. Extended to attachment relationships, this means that children of certain temperaments and parents with certain personalities and/or approaches to parenting don't always form the attachment relationships that we would predict based on these individual characteristics.

Notwithstanding, there is at least some evidence to suggest that shy children are somewhat more likely to develop insecure-resistant attachment relationships. More importantly, however, shy children who do form insecure attachment relationships with their primary caregivers seem to be particularly prone to later difficulties. In contrast, secure attachment relationships can be protective for shy children. For example, researcher Erin Lewis-Morrarty and colleagues (Lewis-Morrarty et al., 2015) tracked a sample of infants until they were teenagers. They found that consistent shyness across childhood was only predictive of anxiety problems in adolescence among children who formed insecure-resistant attachment relationships with their primary caregivers. In contrast, for those children who formed secure attachment relationships, shyness was not predictive of such problems. Thus, a secure relationship with parents served to *buffer* (protect) shy children from later difficulties with anxiety. In contrast, the combination of shyness and an insecure attachment relationship appeared to be a double whammy, resulting in particularly negative outcomes for children.

Attachment theory continues to receive a lot of attention as a primary concept in developmental psychology. As we have just seen, some components of this theory are relevant for the development of shyness in childhood. In particular, it is important for teachers to understand that many shy children may have a general view of the world that is colored by wariness and apprehension. Another relevant branch of research that we need to consider has focused more specifically on the characteristics and socialization patterns of parents that may alter the links between child shyness and anxiety, for better or for worse.

MONKEY SEE, MONKEY DO:
PARENTAL MODELING

In the 1970s, Alfred Bandura proposed *social learning theory* as a primary process by which children learn (Bandura, 1977). This theory states that children observe and model the behaviors, attitudes, and emotional responses of others (think: *monkey see, monkey do*). A caveat to this is that children tend to be particularly influenced by the behaviors of models who are important or prominent to them. So how would this concept apply to parents and their shy children? If parents tend to be more shy themselves, they are likely providing an influential model of "being shy" for their children. This may include modeling shy emotions (e.g., fear, anxiety, embarrassment in certain social situations), cognitions (e.g., verbalizing worries and negative thoughts), and behaviors (e.g., withdrawal, gaze aversion, blushing).

This can have a powerful effect on children, as illustrated by a study by researchers Marci Burstein and Golda Ginsburg (2010). These researchers brought in parents and children to their lab, and children were told that they would be taking two spelling tests. These tests were taken under two different conditions. In one case, parents were trained to act in an anxious manner in anticipation of the test (e.g., rigid posture, twitching, shifting eye gaze, lip-biting). They were also given a script that instructed them to say things like "Oh . . . this test might be too hard for you. I'm worried you won't do well. What if you fail? How embarrassing that would be for you . . . I hope you don't make a fool of yourself!"

In another condition, parents were trained to act in a more confident (nonanxious) manner (e.g., relaxed posture, a positive or neutral facial expression) and were give a script with more positive or optimistic comments about the testing situation, "Oh . . . this test shouldn't be too hard for you. I think you'll do fine. You're going to pass. You should be proud of how you do. I know you'll be able to show them how smart you are."

Right before taking each test, children in both conditions were asked to report how anxious they were feeling, their anxious thoughts, and how much they wanted to avoid taking the test. As you might predict, compared to the confident/nonanxious parent condition, children with a parent acting anxious reported greater anxiety themselves and a stronger desire to avoid the test. Of course, this was a short-term effect based on short-term exposure to parents behaving in a specific manner. As well, this effect was demonstrated in a community sample of children (i.e., not specifically selected for being shy or anxious). Now imagine how this might work for children who are already shy—and who are exposed to such parental behaviors repeatedly and over time! The effects could be quite powerful and long lasting.

DANGER! DANGER! HIGHLIGHTING THREATS

People who are anxious tend to be quick to perceive threats around them—even when situations are ambiguous. Parents who are anxious often have the tendency to highlight such threats to their children. Again, let's illustrate with an exemplary story. Imagine a father and his child kicking a soccer ball together in the park on a sunny weekend afternoon. From a distance, the father sees a teenager walking, carrying a Frisbee, with a large dog trotting beside him. The youth and his dog are gradually approaching where the father and child are playing. At this stage, a nonanxious father might say something like, "Hey, look . . . there's a dog coming."

Now imagine the same scenario, but this time with a more anxious parent and a child who already tends to be somewhat fearful of dogs. Upon noting the approaching dog, such a parent may launch into saying things like, "Okay. . . now don't be afraid . . . but there is a BIG dog coming. It is going to be okay, . . . but I am not sure he is on a leash. So . . . don't touch the dog around his face . . . but it is going to be okay. See, . . . he is getting closer. Let's not make any sudden movements . . . maybe we should stop kicking the ball? It is okay . . . but maybe you should come stand over here near me!"

For shy parents of shy children, we can envision a similar interchange as they arrive for the first day of school ("Okay . . . now don't be nervous . . . there are lots of new kids there . . . they are sure running around a lot and being noisy . . . but it will be important for you to talk to them . . . and to introduce yourself to your teacher . . . but it will be okay . . . are you nervous?"). For shy children who are already prone to be wary, nervous, and self-conscious in such situations, it is not hard to know this might make them feel even more anxious.

There appears to be good reason to pay attention to threat in shy children: heightened sensitivity to threat appears to worsen outcomes for shy children. For example, Koraly Pérez-Edgar and colleagues (2011) found that shyness in toddlerhood (ages 2–3 years) only predicted social difficulties at age 5 years among children who also displayed biases in their attention to threat (that is, when they were more attuned to threat or danger in the environment). Presumably, anything parents can do to reduce their shy child's tendency to perceive things as *dangerous* has the potential to have a positive effect on their social behaviors over time.

PARENTING IN STYLE: PATTERNS OF SOCIALIZATION

In 1975, Diana Baumrind (1975) proposed an extremely influential model of parenting typologies that remains prominent to this day. She suggested that different parents tend to parent according to different *styles*. Parenting styles are general patterns of child-rearing that characterize typical techniques and responses over a broad range of contexts and situations. Baumrind believed that these styles could be identified based on different combinations of parental warmth and control. Let's take a brief look at some of these different styles, with a particular focus on their potential impact for shy children.

Authoritative Parenting

Parents who are high on both warmth and control are labeled as *authoritative*. Parents who engage in authoritative parenting exercise control (e.g., set clear limits) but do so in combination with appropriate levels of warmth, support, acceptance, reasoning, and parent-child communication. Overall, an authoritative parenting style has proven to be generally advantageous to many diverse aspects of children's development. For example, children of authoritative parents tend to have fewer behavior problems and do better academically.

Of particular interest for us, there is some research to suggest that having an authoritative parent may be particularly helpful for shy children. For example, in some of our research (Coplan, Arbeau, & Armer, 2008), we found that shy young children were least likely to have adjustment difficulties at school if they had parents who tended to be more authoritative in their parenting style. Similarly, researchers Kathrine Booth-LaForce and Monica Oxford (2008) found that shy preschoolers tended to become less socially withdrawn over time (preschool to grade 6), when they had mothers who tended to be more supportive and less hostile.

The idea is that parents who are authoritative will provide their shy children with optimal levels of nurturance and support (i.e., high in warmth) but, at the same time, also set and enforce expectations around age-appropriate social behaviors (i.e., high in control). That is, authoritative parents will give their shy children a *push* when needed when it comes to social interactions. However, this will be done in a sensitive and nurturing manner, giving shy children appropriate levels of support to facilitate their efforts. As we will see next, some parents may respond to shy children by pushing too hard—and others by not pushing hard enough.

Authoritarian Parenting

Another socialization style described by Baumrind (1975) was *authoritarian* parenting. Like their authoritative counterparts, authoritarian parents are also high on the dimension of control. However, for authoritarian parents, control is more likely to take the form of rigid enforcement of rules and harsh/punitive discipline. Moreover, authoritarian parents are characterized as being low on warmth. They are more likely to be hostile than nurturing or supportive, and tend not to form an emotional connection with their child. This style of parenting is not only more likely to lead to increased shyness in children, but also to a host of other emotional and behavioral problems.

Let's revisit the case study presented at the beginning of the chapter, which describes parental responses to a child who was scared to go into the pool. In one case, a parent became angry, ignored the child's fear, and then proceeded to throw the child in the swimming pool. This is an example (albeit an extreme one) of authoritarian parenting. It is unlikely that this experience is going to help the child learn how to swim. A scared child thrown into the pool will likely be so overwhelmed by fear and stress that he will not be able to function. Not only that, but the next time he is near a pool—he will likely be even more terrified because of the added worry of having this experience repeat itself. Simply put, if you make a scared child have to *sink or swim,* the child is most likely going to sink!

Now let's adapt this scenario to apply to a shy child on the first day of school. Imagine you are greeting the children in your grade 2 class outside in the yard before bringing them inside to your classroom. Most of the children are assembled. A new child and her mother approach you. The mother introduces the child to you and you kneel down and greet her by name. She does not answer. Instead, she looks away, buries her face in her parent's hip, and starts to cry softly.

Authoritarian parents would be more likely to conceive this type of behavior as disobedient and disrespectful, since their child has *refused* to greet her teacher. They may also believe that such *misbehavior* reflects badly on them as a parent. Under these circumstances, the parent might react to her child's display of shyness with *embarrassment* and *anger*. With this in mind, a typical response from an authoritarian parent would be to attempt to manipulate the child's behaviors in a power-assertive and highly directive fashion (e.g., telling the child how to act or what to say). For example, the parent might chastise the child for her shy behavior and attempt to coerce her into greeting the teacher and going inside to the class. Heightened negative emotional responses from the child, and her continued failure to comply with the parent's demands, could serve to further escalate this situation. This, in turn, could lead to further increases in embarrassment and anger on the part of the parent, which in turn could provoke an even harsher response. Ultimately, the teacher would be left with a very upset and overwhelmed child—who would certainly not be in a good place to begin her first day of school.

This example illustrated what happens when parents of shy children push them too hard. Just like the scared child thrown in the pool, throwing a shy child into social situations (without nurturance and support) will not likely result in learning anything that will help the child feel more comfortable when faced with this type of stress. If anything, this experience will likely only serve to increase the shy child's feelings of fear, anxiety, and worry in social situations. In support of this idea, researchers Booth-LaForce and Oxford (2008), in a study we described earlier, found that shy children who had experienced hostile and unsupportive parenting were increasingly likely to face peer difficulties at school (e.g., dislike, exclusion) and reported more loneliness. As we will discover in the following section, when children lack supportive parenting in stressful social contexts, they tend to be ill-equipped to handle future social situations, including interactions with peers and teachers.

Overprotective Parenting

A pattern of socialization related to development of childhood shyness that has actually received the most attention in recent years is overprotective parenting. This parenting style was not originally specifically identified by Baumrind (1975). Parents who are *overprotective* (sometimes also called *oversolicitous*) tend to overmanage situations for their child, restrict child behaviors, discourage child independence, and direct child activities far more than necessary. There is growing evidence to suggest that shy children tend to evoke overprotective responses from their parents, perhaps because parents wish to ease their children's stress and discomfort. However, as we will see, despite the short-term success that such overprotective strategies may produce in reducing children's immediate stress (and the good intentions on the part of such parents), this parenting style may have long-term negative consequences for shy children.

Going back to the swimming pool example, the parent who responded to the child's fear by taking her home was behaving in a typical overprotective manner. What's more, that child did not learn anything about swimming. In addition, she likely made the connection that there was a good reason to be scared, and that if she is scared, her parent will take her away from what is scaring her, which will alleviate her fear and make her feel better right away. However, the next time and subsequently, when the child is brought to the pool, this scenario is likely to be replayed repeatedly—and she will thus never learn to swim. In this case, the parent was too protective and did not push enough.

How might this apply to the scenario of the shy child on the first day of school? To begin with, overprotective parents tend to perceive their shy children as *vulnerable*. Moreover, such parents may be (or had been) somewhat shy themselves and would tend to strongly identify with their child's shy behaviors. This would potentially result in heightened feelings of worry and anxiety in parents even beforehand, in *anticipation* of the stresses that their shy child will face in this situation.

In the moment, when confronted with a crying child who will not greet his teacher, the parent's immediate goal would likely be to reduce anxiety in the child. This might be done by solving the problem for him (e.g., speaking for the child), attempting to shield the child from stress (e.g., following the child into the classroom), or simply removing the child from the stressful situation (e.g., taking the child home from school). An extremely overprotective parent might even decide that her shy child was not ready for kindergarten and keep him at home for an extra year. The short-term result of overprotective parenting might be a child who appears less upset and distressed. However, under these conditions, the shy child has not learned anything that will help him cope with the next stressful social situation in a more adaptive way. Moreover, what will happen in the future when the mother is not present to deal with the situation? Most likely, the child will be ill-prepared and overwhelmed, and as with the swimming pool example, this will only serve to make the next social encounter that much more stressful.

Shy children may be particularly likely to evoke an overprotective response from parents who tend to be somewhat anxious themselves to begin with. As demonstrated in a study by Ken Rubin and colleagues (Rubin, Nelson, Hastings, & Asendorpf, 1999), mothers who perceived their toddlers as being shy were more likely to change their parenting style and become more overprotective over time. In one of our later studies (Coplan, Reichel, & Rowan, 2009), we found that this effect may be more pronounced among certain types of parents. Our study showed that maternal perceptions of child shyness were most strongly associated with an overprotective parenting style among mothers who were higher in the personality trait of neuroticism. Unfortunately, it seems that this combination of parental characteristics is particularly unhelpful for shy children. Anxious parents are the very parents who are most inclined to be overprotective! In some of our other research (Coplan et al., 2008), we have found that child shyness at the start of kindergarten was most strongly predictive of school adjustment difficulties at the end of the school year among children whose parents themselves tended to be both anxious and overprotective.

Why might this be the case? In short, overprotective parenting is believed to undermine the development of appropriate coping strategies for shy children. Overprotective parents limit or control what their shy children are exposed to, very often intervening to solve social problems for their shy children, or simply removing shy children from challenging social situations. But, of course, parents will not always be able to be there to do this for their shy children (such as all day in the classroom or on the playground). When such shy children are thus thrust into stressful social circumstances like school, they are simply not prepared. Overprotective parenting does not allow shy children to properly develop much-needed self-initiated coping strategies, and this lack of skill, in turn, erodes their self-confidence and perpetuates their feelings of insecurity outside the family. Simply stated, if shy children are never allowed to face their social fears, they will never learn to cope with them.

Lose the Label

A final issue related to parental responses to shyness is a bit of a pet peeve of ours. It is related to the issue of labeling. Some parents are very quick to explicitly label their child as shy in social situations. In the case of the child not introducing himself to the teacher, such a parent would be quick to say something like, "Oh . . . he is just shy." Sometimes other adults (including teachers) will spontaneously do the same thing in front of the child. Regardless of the source, we would suggest that such a practice be avoided for several reasons. First, particularly for younger children, the development of self-concept (one's beliefs about oneself) is heavily influenced by perceptions of important others' views. George Herbert Mead (1934) called this the *looking-glass self*. Basically, children see themselves reflected in how others speak and behave toward them, and then internalize these views as their own. In this regard, the continued use of the shy label by parents and others around the child may contribute to a self-fulfilling prophecy, where the child comes to assume that "if everyone says I am shy" then "I must be shy."

Also, in many ways, simply labeling children as shy essentially *lets them off the hook* in terms of responsibility for their social behaviors. The children are basically provided with a blanket excuse for continuing to act in this manner, without any incentive to alter their behaviors. Instead, shy children must come to realize that there are societal expectations regarding their social behaviors—and that they should be at least trying to work toward a certain level of social facility even in situations in which they are feeling nervous.

So how is this achieved? In our workshops with parents of shy children we give them specific alternative responses to employ when other adults say "oh—is she shy?" For example, parents can explicitly disagree in a good-natured way and with a smile (e.g., "actually no, she is not shy" with a smile) and offer a nonlabeling alternative explanation (e.g., "she just sometimes takes a while to warm up to people she doesn't know, but will introduce herself in a bit"). Such statements establish two important points for shy children. First, that their parents understand and acknowledge their feelings around meeting a new person. Second, and particularly important, such a response establishes an expectation that even if the child is feeling scared, she still needs to at least try to engage socially. We will discuss this strategy as a more general approach to assisting shy children in Chapter 7.

IS THIS CHILD SHY? CAN WE AGREE TO DISAGREE?

As we discussed in Chapter 1, not even developmental psychology researchers can agree exactly on what shyness is and how we should measure it.

With that in mind, it should not come as a surprise that parents and teachers may also have very different perceptions of a specific child's shyness. Indeed, there is only low to modest agreement among parents and teachers regarding children's levels of shyness. These differences can be attributed to several factors.

First, parents and teachers observe children's behaviors in very different contexts. Shy children may appear quite nervous, anxious, and reticent in the stressful environment of the classroom or playing outside during recess (see Chapter 5). However, in the comfortable, familiar, controlled, and comparably *safe* environment of their home, the same children may behave in a much more sociable and interactive manner with their family and close friends. An extreme example of this is the clinical phenomenon of *selected mutism*. Selective mutism is a relatively rare type of anxiety disorder. A child diagnosed with this disorder might persistently fail to speak in specific social situations where speaking is expected (e.g., at school), despite engaging in relatively normative patterns of speaking in other situations (e.g., at home). This discrepant pattern of speech-related behavior would be present for an extended period of time (e.g., beyond the first month of school, during which many children are more reluctant to speak). A parent of a selectively mute child might be shocked to hear from a teacher that the child never talks at school. At the same time, parents see their children's mode of interacting in a variety of settings and with a variety of people, many of whom may be unfamiliar adults. On the other hand, teachers generally see children interacting with other children in the classroom. Although both parent and teacher contexts potentially include stressful situations for shy children, they are different, and the presence of parents provides a source of comfort that is less likely in the classroom (recall our discussion of attachment from earlier in this chapter).

Another reason why parents and teachers may disagree on children's shyness has to do with the nature of shyness itself. As we have seen, a lot of shyness happens on the inside (e.g., thoughts, feelings, motivations). Particularly as children get older, they may become more adept at *hiding* what is going on inside. This may also help to explain why parent and teacher ratings of child shyness can often diverge from children's own self-reports.

Notwithstanding, there has been some interesting research suggesting that it may be important to take a closer look at some of these discrepancies. For example, researchers Andrea Spooner and Mary Ann Evans (Spooner, Evans, & Santos, 2005) studied differences between elementary school children's self-ratings of shyness and ratings made by their parents and teachers. Just over a quarter of the children in the sample self-identified themselves as being shy ("do you consider yourself a shy person?") and also had comparatively high scores on a self-report ratings scale measure of shyness. However, about one third of these self-identified shy children were rated by parents or teachers as *below average* in terms of shyness. That is, one out of three shy children was *undetected* by parents or teachers. Of particular note, those shy children who were mismatched in this way also reported feeling worse about themselves (lower self-esteem) and less confident in their academic abilities (lower perceptions of academic competence) than shy children whom everyone "agreed" were shy. The researchers speculated that children with hidden shyness may not receive enough support and assistance from parents and teachers.

ADVICE FOR TALKING TO PARENTS OF SHY CHILDREN

Drawing upon what we have learned in this chapter, how might teachers seek to better communicate with parents of shy children? There are a couple of general take-home messages that emerge from the developmental psychology literature. First, different parents may respond to shyness in their children in very different ways. Second, parents and teachers may not always agree on whether a given child is shy, since children who are shy at school may not necessarily be shy at home (and vice versa). It is important for teachers to keep both of these points in mind when they are interacting with parents of shy children.

When speaking with *shy parents* of shy children, teachers should be mindful that these parents will likely be worried about their child. Shy parents may over-identify with their shy children and be very motivated to spare their shy child the difficulties that they themselves may have experienced at school growing up. Despite having the very best intentions (and this is important for teachers to understand and acknowledge), shy parents may inadvertently make things worse for their shy child by parenting in an overprotective manner. A good approach with such parents is to talk to them first about classwide goals related to independence and individual accomplishment. Relative to the age of students, this could be linked to independent reading (for children in early elementary, for example) or independent research projects (for those in upper elementary). Starting conversations with parents in this way sets up the importance of teaching independence for all students, without singling out specific students or their parents. This can lead smoothly to a conversation about allowing shy children a chance to flex their social skills, with practice in getting more independent, and having individual accomplishment with additional opportunities to take on new challenges in this area (just as we would with, say, learning to read!).

When speaking to *non-shy parents* of shy children, teachers should be aware that such parents may have difficulty understanding their child's shy behaviors, thoughts, and emotions (their shy child likely responds very differently to the world than they do). As such, if non-shy parents are less sensitive to their shy children's struggles, they may be more likely to push them too hard. Although the conversation with non-shy parents may start out the same as with shy parents of shy children, it may need to take a different tone. In Box 3.1, we list our three favorite books about shyness for you to recommend to parents.

BOX 3.1. THREE BOOKS TO RECOMMEND FOR PARENTS OF SHY AND ANXIOUS CHILDREN

- *Silence Is Not Golden: Strategies for Helping the Shy Child* (Christopher Kearney, 2011, Oxford University Press)
- *Nurturing the Shy Child: Practical Help for Raising Confident and Socially Skilled Kids and Teens* (Barabara G. Markway and Gregory P. Markway, 2006, Thomas Dunne)
- *Key to Parenting Your Anxious Child* (Katharina Manassis, 1996, Barron's Educational Series)

Having spent the previous two chapters exploring the development of shyness from the perspective of nature (e.g., biology, genetics) and nurture (e.g., parenting), in the next chapter we consider why we might, or might not, need to worry about shy children.

CHAPTER 4

Costs and Benefits of Shyness for Children's Development

THE PARABLE OF THE BOLD AND SHY CAVEMEN

Once upon a time there were two cavemen. The first was bold and fearless. Sitting in his cave one day, he felt his stomach grumbling from hunger. Without hesitation, he picked up his spear, strode out of his cave brimming with confidence and enthusiasm, and was promptly eaten by a sabre-toothed tiger that was crouched nearby. He died before having any children.

The second caveman was shy and fearful. When he felt the pangs of hunger, he started inching slowly toward the edge of his cave. However, upon hearing a bush rustle in the wind, he quickly retreated. Later, when he tried again, the shadow of something flying above passed over him as he was about to step out, and he again recoiled. After several additional unsuccessful attempts to leave the cave, he became weak from hunger. Eventually he starved to death, dying without having any children.

After our extensive discussions of what shyness is and how it develops, we now turn to a more detailed consideration of the potential implications of shyness for children at school and beyond. The basic question we address is: *Should we worry about shy children?* In the first part of the chapter, we consider some of the general reasons why we might worry about shy children and some of the specific circumstances that might heighten these concerns. For example, what are the consequences for shy children if they typically spend less time engaging socially with others and more time alone? When shy children inevitably interact with peers at school, how are they typically treated? As compared to their more sociable counterparts, are shy children more likely to develop problems with anxiety and depression? In short, we investigate what developmental psychology might consider as the potential costs of shyness.

Of course, many shy children don't experience difficulties at school and may thrive in this context. Thus, by way of counterpoint, the second part of the chapter features discussions of why we might *not* worry about shy children. For example, in what ways might shyness be adaptive and valued in the classroom from an evolutionary perspective? What specific factors reduce risk and promote success among children? What are some of the more positive aspects of shyness for children? It is our hope that these two perspectives provide a balanced presentation of how shyness influences children's development.

WHY WE MIGHT WORRY ABOUT SHY CHILDREN

On many occasions, we have heard parents lament that our society is *medicalizing* shyness, turning it into a pathology or disease. Such concerns are not without merit, particularly in the face of advertised medications promoted as *cures* for shyness and social anxiety. With that in mind, we feel that it is very important for us to explicitly state that this is not a view that we share. We always try to be clear with parents and teachers that shyness is not something to be changed, cured, or fixed. As we have said herein, shyness is a temperamental trait, a part of one's personality, and part of what makes a child who he or she is.

But, it has also become increasingly clear that there are reasons we should be concerned about *some* shy children. As we will see, research in developmental psychology shows that shyness can contribute to behaviors, feelings, and experiences that are potentially problematic for children. It is thus important for shy children to develop appropriate coping strategies so that their shyness does not prevent them from engaging with their social worlds in ways that will promote their overall well-being. We are mindful not to propagate the message that all shy children are going to have problems. This is simply not true. Our goal here—and throughout this book—is to inform and raise awareness, so that teachers will have the necessary knowledge to apply to the selection of best practices in the classroom. With that said, let's consider some of the reasons why we might want to pay attention to shy children.

The Positive Power of Peers

Children spend almost half of their waking time in the company of peers. As illustrated by the quote in Box 4.1, developmental psychologists have long considered the peer group to be an important and unique context for children's healthy development. Like other important relationships, peers provide children with support, intimacy, and companionship outside of the

---

BOX 4.1. CHILDREN AND CHUMS

All of you who have children are sure that your children love you; when you say that you are expressing a pleasant illusion. If you will look closely at one of your children when he finally finds a chum—somewhere between eight-and-a-half and ten years—you will discover something very different in the relationship, namely that your child begins to develop a real sensitivity to what matters to another person . . . not . . . *what should I do to get what I want* but instead *what should I do to contribute to the happiness or to support the prestige and feeling of worthwhileness of my chum.*

(Harry Stack Sullivan, 1953. p. 245)

---

family environment. However, because of its distinctive nature, the peer group is also a unique source of *learning* for children in many domains.

Because shy children tend to find social situations stressful, they may seek to avoid or withdraw from opportunities for interaction with peers. The end result is that shy children typically end up spending less time talking, interacting, and playing with other children. Thus, if shy children are consistently participating less in this critical setting, they are also missing out on all the benefits that children get from hanging out with friends. What kind of benefits are we talking about? Many of these are related to the characteristics of the peer group that make it different from relationships with parents, teachers, coaches, and other adults.

Imagine a 5-year-old boy who informed his mother that he wanted to take his toy car and go play with it on the highway. He might ask to do this in a very polite and respectful manner, offer elegant and sophisticated arguments for why this was a good thing to do. He might use humor, negotiation, and be extremely persuasive. Yet, no matter how skilled he was in making this request, this is not a debate he is going to win. In fact, if it came down to it, his mother would likely physically restrain him in order to prevent him from running into the road to play in traffic. In contrast, such a socially skilled 5-year-old might very well be able to convince his friend to join him on the road to play with cars!

As this anecdote implies, relationships between children and parents tend to be more *vertical* in nature. That is, as compared to their children, parents basically hold all the cards. They are physically bigger, smarter, more experienced, and have more skills and abilities (even if they do not always feel that way!). This increased power and higher status typically provides them with ultimate authority in dealings with their children, probably at least until adolescence. In contrast, by definition peers are considered equals. Thus, as compared to parent-child and other relationships with adults, peer relationships are more *horizontal* in nature, as the members of these relationships are closer together in terms of their status, power, skills, and abilities. It is the egalitarian nature of peer relationships that seems to help children learn things in this context in different ways than they might from adults.

Sometimes, this learning is in the form of direct communication. In short, peers are clearly a source of distinct information for the child. As they get older, children and adolescents increasingly turn to their peers. Think back when you were growing up. Who did you confide in when it came to sharing your deepest secrets? Who did you ask for advice before a big first date? In many cases, children will talk to peers about things that they may not share with their parents or other adults. This can serve not only as a source of information exchange, but also as a resource for intimacy, empathy, and social support.

Peers are also extremely efficient transmitters of shared group norms, values, and expectations. Over time, many children come to heavily rely on their classmates for input about many aspects of their everyday lives, including how to speak (e.g., expressions, slang), their appearance (e.g., how to dress, hairstyle), and what is in/out in the realm of popular culture (what music to listen to, what movies to see, what is trending in social media). It is this distinct *ethos* shared among social in-groups of peers that creates the so-called *generation gap*.

In their role as general purveyors of social mores, tenets, and customs, peers provide direct and immediate norm-related feedback to children. And there is no question that this feedback carries significant weight. Imagine a mother who bought her 11-year-old new corduroy pants. Many 11-year-old boys are not inherently concerned about their manner of dress or appearance in general. As such, this boy may not think twice about wearing these pants to school one day. However, it turns out that those particularly corduroy pants made "whiff whiff" noises when the boy walked, a phenomenon that was immediately brought to the attention of his classmates. After a day of being laughed at and teased , this boy would be likely to vow to his mother that under no circumstances would he ever wear those pants again. Indeed, he would likely be prepared to suffer any punishment that his mother might have cared to dish out, as long as he could be spared any further negative attention from peers.

The egalitarian nature of peers is also a critical influence in helping children mature in their thinking. As you may recall from Chapter 1, young children are typically very *egocentric* in their views (that is—they can only see things from their own perspective). Overcoming these self-centered biases is a major cognitive task of early childhood. The peer group is an ideal context for challenging such egocentric views. Routine social experiences in the classroom and on the playground expose children to a wide range of diverse views, abilities, beliefs, and characteristics. Such exchanges help to highlight for children the immense variety of likes, dislikes, and alternative opinions that populate their social realms. Over time, this repeated exposure helps to eat away at the rigid walls of egocentrism and promote children's abilities to understand diverse views and take on others' perspectives.

The peer group is also an essential realm for the development of children's emerging self-concepts. Young children are typically not very good at judging their own characteristics, abilities, strengths, or weaknesses as compared to others. For example, an entire class of kindergarten children may put their hands up enthusiastically when asked "who is the fastest runner?" or "who is the smartest?" In Chapter 3, we mentioned the notion of the *looking-glass self*, whereby children's emerging self-concept is heavily influenced by how they are treated and responded to by important others. Entrance into the peer group provides children with multiple and immediate sources of feedback that help to shape their developing sense of self. This feedback promotes comparison with peers, who are both similar to the child (and clearly more similar than adults) but also noticeably different in important and meaningful ways. This builds children's capacities for considering their own distinctness within a broader social context.

Thus, peers provide *all* children with unique experiences, exposures, and interactions that shape their evolving social views, both about themselves and about others. Of course, when individuals with different perspectives, priorities, and personalities come into contact, differences of opinions, disagreements, and direct conflicts can also emerge. In many cases, however, these encounters provide children with invaluable opportunities to acquire and hone emerging social skills. Indeed, it is with peers that children are most likely to learn lifelong lessons in cooperation, turn-taking, negotiation, conflict resolution, and the rest of the tools we need for competent, successful, and effective social interactions.

Like any other abilities, the mastery of such social skills requires practice, practice, practice! As a result, children who spend less time *practicing* (i.e., interacting with peers) will likely lag behind in terms of the acquisition and mastery of these skills. Moreover, this deficit is likely to be cumulative. It is like missing the first 3 weeks of math class. Even if you were good at math to begin with, you will have difficulty following what is being covered in class right now, which may cause you to fall even farther behind.

Similarly, over time social skills deficits are likely to cumulate, making it more difficult for such children to engage positively with peers. In turn, this will make their growing gap in social skills even wider, which will make them even less likely to get optimal levels of social interactions, and so on. Many shy children are already prone to withdraw from and avoid opportunities for peer interaction because of the stresses that such situations evoke for them. Thus, it may be particularly important to monitor the frequency of shy children's peer interactions, in order to make sure that they have adequate opportunities to take advantage of all of the good stuff that children can get from peers. However, as we will see in the next section, along with the quantity, it will also be important to be attentive to the *quality* of shy children's interactions with peers.

Sticks, Stones, and Words Can Hurt Me

School is a social environment. For shy children, meeting new children, working on a group project with classmates, speaking in front of the class, and approaching playmates on the playground all represent potential sources of stress. Many shy children find themselves under-prepared for dealing with these stresses, and, feeling overwhelmed, will seek to withdraw and minimize the frequency of their social encounters. Over time, this poses its own set of concerns for children's development. However, even if shy children seek to avoid direct engagement, throughout the school day they are almost always in the presence of peers. And, of course, these other children are more than just passive observers of shy children's behaviors. Unfortunately, the responses that shy children often evoke from their classmates are not always so positive.

Why might peers react negatively to shy children? Well, to begin with, shy children's behaviors may draw the wrong kind of attention from peers. For example, if you wanted to quickly identify a potentially shy child in your class, the most reliable way to do this would probably be to look for a child off by herself. Now, in early childhood, it is quite common for children to play alone in the presence of peers. Social exchanges in preschool and kindergarten are often brief and inconsistent, and children are probably more likely to play in parallel (next to, but not *with* others) than they are to engage in true joint and cooperative play. Thus, shy young children may not *stick out* as much if they are simply engaging in fewer social interactions.

However, as children get older, social interactions with peers increase in both frequency and sophistication. And, as discussed earlier in this chapter, social interactions with peers become more important. For these reasons, shy children's solitary behaviors in the presence of peers increasingly violate rising social norms and expectations. Undeniably, by late childhood, peer interaction is expected by default. This is illustrated in one of our recent studies (Coplan, Ooi, & Rose-Krasnor, 2015) that included extensive observations of 10- to 12-year-old children's social behaviors on the playground during recess and lunch. We found that, on average, children spent more than 90% of their time playing with or talking to one or more peers. This may help explain why being *alone* at recess or lunch is universally identified by school-age children as one of the most socially awkward and embarrassing experiences.

So, over time, shy children's tendencies for solitary activities will likely become viewed as increasingly deviant by classmates. There is also research to suggest that shy children are more likely to be disliked, excluded, and victimized by peers, even at early ages. This may be because shy children are not just playing alone, but they are also displaying other behaviors that may single them out among their peers in a way that may invite negative responses.

As we have already mentioned, shy children are thought to experience an internal motivational conflict between their desire to play with others and the fear/anxiety that social situations evoke. As a result, a common behavior of shy children in social contexts is *onlooking* (hovering near where others are playing, watching but not joining in). Similarly, overwhelmed by social fear and self-consciousness, shy children sometimes simply remain unoccupied among peers, wandering around aimlessly or staring off into space. This pattern of onlooking and remaining unoccupied in the presence of peers is called *reticent behavior.*

Results from several studies indicate that reticent behaviors are not perceived positively by peers, even in early childhood. For example, in one study (Coplan, Girardi, Findlay, & Frohlick, 2007) we presented young children with vignettes depicting hypothetical classmates displaying a variety of common classroom social behaviors. One thing we learned was that children tended to view the hypothetical reticent child as a less appealing potential playmate compared to more sociable classmates. In another study with *actual* peers conducted by researcher Xinyin Chen and colleagues (Chen, DeSouza, Chen, & Wang, 2006), quartets of previously unfamiliar 4-year-old children were observed interacting in a laboratory playroom. It was found that when one child displayed reticent behavior, then other children were less likely to respond with positive behaviors such as approval and cooperation, and were more likely to respond with acts of rejection such as overt refusal and disagreement. We found similar results in another of our studies conducted at school, with children's reticent behavior in kindergarten predicting peer rejection and other social difficulties over the course of the school year (Coplan et al., 2008).

So, even when they are not directly interacting with peers, shy children's behaviors may invite negative views and responses. But, of course, even though shy children are less likely to initiate social bids, they do not spend *all* of their time alone at school. However, when they do interact directly with others, shy children tend to be less socially skilled. Research has shown that shy children display fewer positive and prosocial behaviors among peers, are less assertive, and tend to have less developed social-communicative skills. Moreover, these associations persist throughout childhood. For example, in one study, Gunilla Bohlin and colleagues (Bohlin, Hagekull, & Andersson, 2005) found that shyness at age 4 predicted lower social competence and popularity among peers at school 4 years later. In another longer-term study, Evalill Karevold and colleagues (Karevold, Ystrøm, Coplan, Sanson, & Mathiesen, 2012) reported that shyness in early childhood predicted poorer social skills in adolescence.

Some researchers have also looked more specifically at the friendships of shy children. Friends serve many positive functions for children and are important sources of support, nurturance, intimacy, and companionship. The good news is that shy children are not necessarily any less likely than others to have a close friend in their class. However, not all friendships are created equal—and shy children appear to be more likely to form friendships of lesser quality.

Research by Kenneth Rubin and colleagues (Rubin, Wojslawowicz, Rose-Krasnor, Booth-LaForce, & Burgess, 2006) suggests that shy children tend to form friendships with one another and with children who are targets of bullying. Moreover, when they do make friends, the friendships of shy children were found to be lower in intimacy, have less helping and guidance, and be poorer in conflict resolution compared to friendships of more sociable children. This pattern may start as early as preschool, which means that shy children may have long-term trajectories of less than optimal experiences with friendship and peers in general, and this may hurt their social skill development, as discussed earlier in this chapter.

Part of these social difficulties may be explained by a deficit in social *competence*. This would be in keeping with the *lack of practice makes lack of perfect* effect that we talked about previously. However, it has also been suggested that even if shy children do know what to say and how to act in social settings, they may not be able to demonstrate this knowledge. This would be more of a *performance* deficit. Shy children may fail to enact competent and effective social strategies and behaviors because they are simply too scared or self-conscious, or because they lack confidence in their social abilities.

Unfortunately, regardless of underlying causes, a behavioral profile characterized by poorer social skills, solitary activities, and a submissive nature is a further cause for concern because it may invite the attention of bullies. Indeed, some research suggests that children who are most frequently victimized by their peers tend to be less sociable, more socially withdrawn, more submissive, and have fewer leadership skills (Perren & Alsaker, 2006). It has been suggested that because they are less likely to fight back, shy children might be perceived as *easy marks* for bullies.

Children who experience fewer and lower quality peer relations are at risk for a host of negative social, emotional, and academic outcomes. This gives us good reason to keep a close eye on all children who are struggling socially. However, it may be particularly important to do this in the case of children who are shy. Research by Heidi Gazelle and Gary Ladd (2003) suggests that shy children are particularly vulnerable to the negative consequences of consistent peer difficulties. Over the course of one 5-year longitudinal study, these researchers found that shy children in kindergarten who experienced consistent peer exclusion over time displayed the most stable shyness through grade 4 and were also at the highest risk for developing symptoms of depression.

By way of explanation, there is some evidence that shy children's typical coping strategies for dealing with stressful peer experiences may contribute to their vulnerability. In one study (Kingsbury, Coplan, & Rose-Krasnor, 2013), we asked children ages 9 to 13 how likely they would be to use different types of coping strategies if they were to have a fight with a friend. Shy children were more likely to report that they would use *emotion-focused* strategies, that is, coping attempts characterized by avoidance and rumination ("go off by myself"; "cry about it"). In turn, the more frequent use of emotion-focused strategies was related to greater symptoms of anxiety and depression.

Taken together, all of this paints a potentially worrisome picture for shy children based on their peer group experiences. This is clearly a domain that merits teachers' attention at school. In Chapter 8, we will discuss specific strategies that teachers can use to foster more positive peer experiences for shy children. We now turn our attention to some of the *bad feelings* that may accompany or result from these negative peer experiences for shy children at school.

Not Feeling Alright

Shy children enter the school environment already prone to feelings of fear, self-consciousness, and anxiety. The stresses of the classroom and the possible negative experiences with peers can serve to further aggravate these already existing tendencies to *feel bad*. From early childhood to adolescence, results from many studies have linked higher levels of shyness with more negative self-perceptions and the heightened experience of negative emotions, including loneliness, anxiety, sadness, and other internalizing problems.

Feelings of self-doubt, a lack of confidence, self-consciousness, and concerns about how others see them can lead shy children to feel poorly about themselves. For example, in one study (Crozier, 1995), shy elementary school children were found to report lower overall self-esteem than their more sociable classmates, as well as less positive perceptions of their social and scholastic competence. It is important to note here that shy children are not just feeling less positive about their social realms, but these negative views extend to other domains, such as their perceived academic abilities, and contribute toward more general feelings of lower self-worth. Moreover, these negative views appear to start even in early childhood, despite young children's general tendency to *overestimate* their abilities. In one of our studies (Coplan, Findlay, & Nelson, 2004), we found that the shyest 4- to 5-year-old children also reported the lowest perceptions of their own physical and scholastic competence.

It is not hard to envision why shy children might feel lonely in the peer group. As we have already described, despite a desire to play with others, shy children typically end up interacting less with peers, either because of withdrawing from or avoiding opportunities for social exchanges, or because they are actively excluded from such opportunities by other children. By definition, loneliness represents a discrepancy between the levels of social engagement that we would like compared to the levels that we actually have. If shy children are not managing to connect with peers enough to satisfy their social wants and needs, this will serve to worsen their feelings of loneliness and social dissatisfaction.

So, taken together, these research findings suggest that shy children may be more likely to develop negative feelings about themselves and their place in the social world. Over time, low self-esteem and loneliness can foster feelings of anxiety and depression. *This is perhaps the most concerning potential long-term risk of extreme shyness in childhood.*

There is growing evidence that childhood shyness is a substantive risk factor for the later development of more serious mental health difficulties. The most well-established link is from childhood shyness to adolescent anxiety. There have been several studies showing that extremely shy children are prone to problems with anxiety, both at the sub-clinical level (that is, heightened symptoms, but not high enough to warrant a formal diagnosis) and in terms of diagnosed anxiety disorders. For example, research by Andrea Chronis-Tuscano and colleagues (2009) found that children who were consistently extremely shy from ages 1 to 7 were four times more likely than non-shy children to have been diagnosed with an anxiety disorder at some point in their lives.

The biggest risk appears to be for developing social anxiety disorder (Clauss & Blackford, 2012). Social anxiety disorder is most typically diagnosed in early adolescence, but diagnoses in younger children are becoming more common. Childhood social anxiety disorder is associated with a wide range of negative outcomes, including academic impairment, disrupted social relationships, school refusal, somatic symptoms, substance abuse, depression, and other psychiatric problems. Overall, extremely shy children are on average about seven times more likely than non-shy children to be later diagnosed with social anxiety disorder.

We struggled here with how to present this information in a sensible way. On the one hand, these statistics are quite worrisome. Social anxiety is a debilitating mental health problem that can greatly interfere with individuals' day-to-day lives, at home, at work, and in relationships. People with social anxiety are also more likely to develop depression. Moreover, despite these pervasive and disruptive effects, barriers such as stigma and costs prevent most people with social anxiety from seeking effective available treatments. Thus, we do not want to minimize the importance of identifying and assisting those shy children who may be on pathways toward these serious mental health difficulties.

As an important counterpoint, however, we must note that although childhood shyness may help to shape later development, this influence is not rigid nor is it consistently negative. Many factors contribute to children's developing well-being. The probabilities and risks reported in the aforementioned studies must be interpreted in context. Indeed, Nathan Fox and colleagues (Fox, Henderson, Marshall, Nichols, & Ghera, 2005) have emphasized that at least half of extremely shy children do *not* go on to experience problems with anxiety. With this mind, we now more explicitly consider some of the reasons why we might *not* worry about shy children

WHY WE MIGHT *NOT* WORRY ABOUT SHY CHILDREN

As we mentioned at the outset of Chapter 1, over 80% of adults consider themselves to be or to have been shy at one time. Yet most adults who were shy as children would likely report that they turned out just fine. How can we reconcile the normative nature of shyness with the increased risks for negative outcomes that it apparently imposes? This is the difficult balance that we are trying to achieve in this chapter. For all the reasons we just explored, and likely more, we should worry about some shy children—but not all shy children. In fact, in some cases it could be quite the opposite. Some shy children thrive at school and may benefit from this aspect of their personality. Accordingly, we now consider some of the potentially more positive facets of shyness.

Adaptively Shy

To start, let's revisit the cavemen parable presented at the outset of this chapter. It provides a greatly over-simplified depiction of an evolutionary perspective on personality dimensions such as shyness-boldness. Notwithstanding, it is meant to illustrate that people who are bold can sometimes be too bold in potentially dangerous situations. In contrast, people who are shy can sometimes be too shy to take advantage of important opportunities. Thus, the moral of the story is that it is probably a good thing for humanity in general that not all of us turned out to be extremely bold or extremely shy.

Evolutionary approaches consider the *adaptive* nature of traits and characteristics at the level of a species. An adaptive trait is something that grants a subset of organisms who share this characteristic any kind of advantage that promotes their survival. Surviving longer in turn generally provides these specific organisms with greater opportunities to mate and pass on this trait to subsequent generations. A classic example illustrates how this process resulted in giraffes evolving to have longer necks. Individual giraffes who happened to be born with a gene that results in a slightly longer neck will have an advantage over their shorter-necked brethren in procuring food because they can reach higher up trees to eat more leaves. Over time, this success led to greater survival rates and more offspring sired by giraffes with longer necks, until this characteristic eventually became the norm in the species.

As you might expect, things are much more complicated when it comes to general adaptive value of personality traits and our specific two cavemen in question. As it turns out, under different circumstances, both boldness and shyness may be advantageous. For example, bold cavemen may be more favored and successful when competing for resources such as food and mates, particularly when such resources are scarce. Evidence for these assertions can be found in research with animals. For example, one study (Boyce, O'Neill-Wagner, Price, Haines, & Suomi, 1998) looked at the effect of overcrowding on a troop of Rhesus Macaques. Under normal living conditions, there was relatively little violent conflict within monkey troops, and shy versus bold monkeys shared the same relatively low incidence of injuries. However, when placed in more stressful conditions (in this case, overcrowded confinement), it was the shy monkeys who suffered the most injuries from the resulting increase in conflicts.

In contrast, shy cavemen may be more adept at avoiding predators. In environments of heightened threat, the tendency to look before you leap will be of extremely high value. Moreover, shyness may have positive adaptive functions in certain social contexts. For example, researcher Cristina Colonnesi (Colonnesi, Napoleone, & Bögels, 2014) suggests that some behavioral displays of shyness (such as a *coy* smile—which involves the combination of smiling, avoiding eye contact, and tilting the head) can reduce social tension in potentially stressful social situations (like meeting a stranger). This is because these behavioral responses are typically perceived as nonthreatening and prosocial and thus induce trust.

Crucially, humans evolved in complex, unpredictable, and rapidly changing environments. For this reason and many others, the best chance for survival and successful continued adaptation for humanity as a whole was to have a wide range of shyness and boldness represented and distributed among the members of the species. Thus, from an evolutionary perspective, shyness is inherently neither good nor bad. It offers advantages and disadvantages in different contexts—and it is optimal for humans (including children) to vary along the full dimensional range on this trait.

Shy But Doing Fine

Given the wide range of possible outcomes associated with childhood shyness, developmental psychologists have sought to uncover some of the reasons why some shy children *do better* than others over time. Such protective factors serve to buffer shy children from some of the risks that we have previously discussed. Identifying naturally occurring protective factors in different domains can also shed some light on potentially effective target areas for early intervention and prevention efforts.

We saw some examples of this in Chapter 3 from the domain of parenting. Parental responses that combine warmth and support with appropriate levels of encouragement and incentive may be particularly helpful in improving social outcomes for shy children. Similarly, positive parent-child attachment relationships appear to reduce fear and encourage social exploration in shy children.

This type of research has led to significant advancements in the development of education and training specifically targeted for parents of young and extremely shy children. For example, researcher Ron Rapee and colleagues (Rapee, Kennedy, Ingram, Edwards, & Sweeney, 2005) presented one group of mothers of extremely shy preschoolers with a six-session parent-education program about how anxiety develops, techniques to help children manage anxiety, and techniques for parents to manage their own anxiety. A second group of mothers of similarly shy children who did not receive the program served as the comparison group. One year later, shy children whose mothers received the program demonstrated a substantively greater reduction in anxiety than children in the comparison group. In a follow-up study (Rapee, 2013), this brief early intervention program for parents of shy preschoolers was still found to be demonstrating benefits in reducing children's anxiety 11 years later in mid-adolescence!

Other research has focused on individual characteristics and abilities that may promote resiliency in the shy child. The idea here is that there are other traits that might generally promote positive outcomes in all children, but they could be particularly critical factors in the well-being of shy children. One good example of this is in the domain of language skills. In a series of studies (Coplan & Armer, 2005; Coplan & Weeks, 2009), we looked at the protective role of linguistic and communicative skills (e.g., vocabulary, pragmatics) for shy children. We found that although better language skills are generally associated with more positive social outcomes for all children, they play a particularly important function for shy children. For children with better language skills, shyness was no longer associated with negative outcomes such as peer exclusion.

Think of it like this. If you are extroverted and exuberant and you want to talk to someone, it will probably not slow you down too much if the right words don't always come easily for you. You will likely just push on with your best efforts to make yourself understood. In contrast, if you are shy and you struggle with language, this would be a particularly debilitating combination for social encounters. However, if you are shy and approach social exchanges with trepidation, imagine how potentially helpful it might be to have a facility with language. Having that important social tool could go a long way toward facilitating your social interactions over time.

As well, researchers have identified other traits that seem to function similarly for shy children and adolescents. For example, in one study (Gazelle, 2008), prosocial characteristics such as being cooperative and a good listener appeared to be particularly influential in improving shy children's acceptance in the peer group. In another study (Markovic & Bowker, 2015), having a good sense of humor promoted better peer outcomes for shy adolescents (particularly girls). As we will see in Chapter 7, this type of research has led to the recent development of social skills training programs specifically targeted for young shy children, with promising preliminary results.

Positively Shy

In the face of the mounting evidence linking shyness with negative outcomes presented in the first part of this chapter, there are clearly reasons to be potentially worried about some shy children. However, as we have seen in the latter part of this chapter, many shy children do just fine. Taken together, all of this research reminds us that shyness does not define children—it is but one aspect of their personality.

Moreover, as we have seen, this facet of their personality may have some benefits. Shy children have been described as good listeners, easier to approach, and as having a calming influence on others. Shy children may also be more sensitive to their environments, which can promote attention to detail and insight. Shy children may also benefit from some of the time they spend in solitude. Solitary endeavors can promote creativity, mastery, and productivity. Solitude also offers valuable opportunities for self-reflection and examination. And, of course, history is filled with countless examples of extremely successful thinkers (Charles Darwin, Albert Einstein), leaders (Abraham Lincoln, Mahatma Gandhi), and creators (Ludwig Van Beethoven, Andy Warhol) who "grew up shy." Indeed, as we will see in the next chapter, there are several reasons why shyness may have specific positive benefits in the classroom.

CHAPTER 5

Shy Children in the Classroom

CASE STUDY: QUIET ON THE OUTSIDE, NOISY ON THE INSIDE

In the back row of his grade 6 math class, Juan appears to be sitting quietly as his teacher reviews a complex example on the blackboard. However, inside Juan's head, things are far from quiet. He worries what will happen if the teacher suddenly called upon him to answer a question.

Even though he is generally good at math, he is worried that he will not know the answer, or that he will fluster when he has to talk. What if the teacher gets angry with him? Will the teacher think he is stupid? Will he get a bad grade? What if his face goes red and everyone in the class looks at him? Will the other kids make fun of him? Will his friends not like him anymore? Will that mean that he will not have anyone to sit with at lunch today?

Juan's racing thoughts are interrupted when the teacher erases the blackboard and announces that the period is over. Juan looks down at the paper in front of him and realizes he did not take any notes. . . .

As this case study illustrates, shyness can affect a child's experiences in the classroom in subtle ways. At the same time, although shy children may seem calm or fine on the outside (or even go completely unnoticed), inside they are likely feeling quite different (worrying about what is coming next, whether the teacher will ask them a question, who they will sit with at lunch, etc.). This internal storm of thoughts and feelings can have significant implications for shy children's experiences in the classroom.

Based on what we know about shyness and how it develops, it is clear that shy children's behavior and academic performance in the classroom is likely to be different from that of their less shy peers. Understanding how shy children's behavior unfolds in a classroom setting is particularly useful so that teachers can more easily identify shy children. Indeed, many teachers are *not* shy, so it may be difficult to see certain behaviors as *rooted* in shyness. For example, a child who looks down when she's asked a question by her teacher ("Did you take Joey's pencil?") may appear to be guilty when, in fact, she is afraid of being viewed negatively by the teacher (and, potentially, peers who may be watching).

In this chapter, we highlight what typically happens to shy children in the classroom, a context with characteristics that can be particularly stressful for them. We begin with a discussion of why the classroom environment might be demanding for shy children. Then we consider how shy children's feelings, thoughts, and behaviors in the classroom might impact their academic success. As we saw in the previous chapter, there appear to be both potential costs and benefits for shy children in the classroom.

WHY IS THE CLASSROOM STRESSFUL FOR SHY CHILDREN?

It is certainly not unreasonable for teachers to expect the children in their classrooms to adapt to the demands of this unique environment. However, our general approach to schooling and many common aspects of pedagogy were certainly not designed with shy children in mind! Given what we have learned already about shy children's temperament, biology, and thought processes, it is not hard to imagine typical experiences and demands of the school context that might cause them particular stress (Coplan & Arbeau, 2008; Kalutskaya, Archbell, Rudasill, & Coplan, 2015). A partial list is provided in Box 5.1.

**BOX 5.1. COMMON CIRCUMSTANCES
THAT MAY EVOKE SHYNESS IN CHILDREN AT SCHOOL**

- Meeting new people and entering new social environments (e.g., first day of school)
- Large groups of children
- Show-and-tell
- Being the center of attention
- Being called on in class
- Presenting in front of others
- Receiving praise
- Receiving invitations to play from other children
- Interacting with people in authority
- Interacting with a member of the opposite sex (or any potential romantic partner)
- Finding a group or partner for a class activity
- Having someone to sit with at lunchtime

Classrooms can certainly be demanding environments for many children. There are general expectations that children will listen to their teachers, behave as instructed, and interact with peers for academic and social purposes. As such, classrooms are *social* environments. As we have seen, the mere presence of peers is a source of potential stress for shy children. In addition, a common expectation by both teachers and peers in classrooms is that children will verbally participate in class activities. This might include answering questions in front of the class, making an oral presentation, working with peers in small groups, and initiating conversations with the teacher when needed (such as asking questions about content or instructions). However, many of these expectations are particularly difficult for shy children to meet because of characteristics inherent in most elementary classrooms: There is constant change and novelty, peers are always present, and the teacher is an authority figure (and therefore can be intimidating).

New Things Can Be Scary

Shy children are usually most comfortable in familiar and predictable environments. Despite efforts by teachers to establish regular routines, typical elementary classrooms remain places where shy children encounter new people and unfamiliar situations on a regular basis. As we have seen, novelty is a common trigger of wariness and unease for shy children. This is particularly notable at the start of the school year. The context of entering a new class typically presents multiple stressors, including the unfamiliarity and uncertainty that comes with having a new teacher, classroom, peers, rules, procedures, and expectations. Moreover, although many shy children may be simply *slow to warm up* (as we discussed in Chapter 1), there can be quite a bit of variation in the length of the warm-up period. For example, although some shy children may start to feel more comfortable after the first few hours, for others it may take days or even weeks to come out of their shells. These issues will likely be most disruptive during the first year of formal school (kindergarten) or after the transition to a new school. However, any transition to a new classroom and teacher (even with many familiar kids) may prove to be particularly stressful for shy children.

As the school year progresses, shy children are still likely to confront many new situations and experiences in the classroom. For example, the social context of the classroom may change with the arrival of a substitute (or replacement) teacher or a new classmate. Daily routines may change, such as having lunch in the classroom rather than the lunchroom. Students may be expected to complete a group project and present it to the class or learn something new and demanding, such as how to diagram sentences. The class may go on a field trip and be assigned with a group of peers to a chaperon that they have never met before. Students may have to perform in front of the school in a class production. Certain types of these new experiences will likely be more or less stressful to different shy children (some will be most worried about having a new teacher, others more about learning new material, still others about talking in front of the class). Moreover, classrooms often continue to change throughout the school year because there is pressure on teachers to provide a vibrant and stimulating environment. As a result, a more dynamic environment is often encouraged (Keep the kids moving! Invite guest speakers! Have the children work in groups!). However, this can be at the cost of the comfort of shy children, who are more at home when the environment is predictable and familiar.

Thus, change and novelty are inevitable in the elementary classroom, and continue to regularly occur well beyond the beginning of the school year. This means that for many shy children, the stresses of the school environment do not just go away after the first days or weeks of school. This was well illustrated by researchers Sara Rimm-Kaufman and Jerome Kagan (2005), who repeatedly observed children's behaviors in class in kindergarten. They found that shy children's behaviors (e.g., speaking less than non-shy children) remained quite stable and consistent over the course of several months. Results from several other studies support this assertion as well. For example, as we saw in Chapter 4, shy children display a tendency to withdraw from peer interactions throughout the school year. Thus, the classroom environment is not only intimidating to shy children at the beginning of a new school year, but also potentially at points of change throughout the school year.

Other Children Can Be Scary

One of the key points of stress for shy children in the classroom is that most classroom activities happen in the presence of peers. Indeed, even after classmates become familiar and everyday companions, they may still be a source of stress for shy children. Thus, the mere *presence* of peers in the classroom can be intimidating for shy children. Shy children are often overly concerned about how others see them and are prone to self-consciousness. As such, they may be reluctant to answer questions or speak in front of the group. In Chapter 4, we discussed the peer difficulties shy children experience that may amplify feelings of anxiety, loneliness, and stress in the classroom because they are not getting along well with, or feeling supported by, other children in the class.

The differences in the ways that shy children engage in the classroom may be most pronounced during whole-class or large-group contexts where the teacher is leading. This is consistent with the idea that being in front of a group (i.e., having an audience) makes shy children uneasy. Indeed, sociable and bold children (i.e., not shy) tend to speak in class almost twice as often as their shy peers in these large- or whole-group classroom settings. Given the inherent social and dynamic nature of the classroom, it is easy to see how this environment may seem unfriendly to a shy child, and may heighten a child's level of stress. One context where this is often seen is during the common early childhood classroom practice of *show-and-tell*. Let's imagine this scenario from the perspective of a shy child, where it will be clear that this represents such a child's worst nightmare!

It is time for show-and-tell in 1st grade. Most of the children are excited. This is the chance to bring something special from home (a toy, a picture, a memento) to show to the class, and to talk about why it is special. The teacher requires that each child participates, and this means not only asking other children about what they have brought, but also bringing something to share. Although this has many appealing qualities and teaches children important skills such as taking turns, questioning, showing interest, and listening, it has a specific combination of characteristics that make it a uniquely stressful activity for shy children. For shy children, this "fun" activity involves: (1) being in a large group of peers (whose presence can be stressful); (2) standing up and being the center of attention; (3) having to talk in front of everyone (including answering questions from the teacher); and (4) being watched and evaluated by the teacher. This is more than enough stress to cause most shy children to completely shut down. As a result, this dreaded activity often plays out with shy children speaking very quietly, briefly, or not at all. Moreover, teachers often respond to shy children's silence by asking a lot of follow-up questions (adding to an already stressful queue of unanswered questions in shy children's minds) or by becoming impatient or frustrated. As such, this entire experience can prove to be very painful for shy children, likely worsening any anxiety they already have about school, peers, teachers, and the classroom.

Teachers Can Be Scary Too

Teachers, the cornerstone of the elementary classroom environment, may also be intimidating to shy children because they are sources of power, authority, and evaluation. Indeed, for some shy children it may be teachers, not peers, who are the primary source of stress; in this case the signs of shyness may be less easily recognizable. A parent once provided a good example of this when she described her daughter's experience at school. This child was generally very sociable, and, after a bit of a warm-up period, made friends easily. However, adults tended to make her quite nervous, particularly *certain* adults. This seemed to have to do with positions of authority in general (i.e., being a teacher), but was also affected by the nature of the adult (e.g., the way in which the adult interacted with her). Thus, when the teacher was warm and friendly, her daughter was less likely to be intimidated and more quickly put at ease (although she might still be a bit worried about negative evaluation, and would never want the teacher to view her badly). When the teacher was stern, she was more intimidated and displayed all of the signs of shyness that we would expect, such as avoiding eye contact and few verbal responses. As we will see in the next chapter, the way that shy children behave in front of teachers may lead to less positive teacher-child relationships and more negative teacher attitudes.

The special position that teachers have (and perhaps why they wield such power in the lives of children) is that they are in the business of *evaluating* children all the time, both in formal (as in testing) and informal ways. Since shy children tend to be excessively concerned about evaluation, teachers can become a source of great intimidation and stress. Yet, teachers generally expect children to come to them with questions or problems, and encourage children to engage in classroom activities through opportunities to share and present information to others (such as show-and-tell, partner reading, and group projects). However, pushing shy children to speak up, particularly in front of an audience, appears to only have the effect of increasing their reluctance to speak. As we indicated earlier, show-and-tell can be a painful activity for shy children for multiple reasons.

Researcher Mary Ann Evans (Evans & Bienert, 1992) conducted extensive observations of shy and non-shy children during show-and-tell. She found that when teachers used a high-control style, characterized by repetitive questioning, shy children spoke very little. In contrast, shy children spoke more frequently during show-and-tell when teachers used a low-control style, which included asking fewer questions and making more explanatory comments. With this in mind, we will see in Chapter 8 that there are specific techniques that teachers can employ to improve relationships with shy children and increase their verbal participation in the classroom. Having established why the classroom may be particularly stressful for shy children, we now take a look at how shyness might impact children's academic performance at school.

SHYNESS AND ACADEMIC PERFORMANCE

Shyness is not related to intelligence. That is, there is no research evidence to suggest that shy and non-shy children differ in terms of their general IQ. However, there have been a number of studies demonstrating that, overall, shy children tend to do less well academically as compared to their less-shy classmates (e.g., Coplan & Evans, 2009; Crozier & Hostettler, 2003; Hughes & Coplan, 2010). Reasons for this appear to be quite complex. For example, consider how shy students typically behave in the classroom. As detailed in Box 5.2, shy children tend to be quiet and may even seem unwilling or reluctant to engage in classroom discussions or activities. Some of our research has shown that shy children are less likely than their peers to receive teacher-initiated interactions in class. They may also freeze-up if called on by the teacher and will typically be uninterested in volunteering

---

BOX 5.2. COMMON BEHAVIORS OF SHY CHILDREN AT SCHOOL

- Refusal to speak
- Speaking quietly or briefly
- Not volunteering to speak in a group
- Avoiding eye contact/looking down or away
- Blushing
- Developing a rash on the face/neck
- Hunched posture
- Watching other children but not joining in
- Hovering on the edge of where other children are playing or talking
- Playing or doing some other activity (e.g., reading) alone in the presence of other children (social withdrawal)
- Turning down invitations to play or interact with other children
- Overt anxious behaviors (e.g., crying, biting nails, playing with own hair)
- Clinging to parent, teacher, or comfort object

---

responses to teacher questions (instead, waiting for more sociable children to jump in!). One result of this lack of engagement may be that shy children receive smaller "doses" of teacher attention, instruction, and interaction, which may hinder their learning in class. A complete discussion of shy children and teachers is provided in the next chapter. In the following sections, we consider some of the other factors that have been found to contribute to shy children's academic underperformance.

Difficulties with Classroom Engagement

Beyond reducing direct contact with teachers, shy children's inability or reluctance to participate in classroom activities may also hinder the acquisition of skills and knowledge in the classroom. Classroom *engagement* (showing on-task behavior, interest, enthusiasm) is a crucially important contributor to children's academic achievement. Indeed, results from several studies have identified engagement as a better indicator of children's success in school than either grades or performance on achievement tests. This is thought to be because high levels of engagement demonstrate motivation to succeed that will have lasting and positive effects. Thus, hindrances to children's engagement in classroom instructional activities can be particularly problematic.

Lack of engagement appears to be an important part of the mechanism that connects shyness with lower achievement. In our research with upper elementary students, we found that shy children were perceived by teachers as being less engaged in academic activities, and that this lower engagement was, in turn, related to poorer academic achievement (Hughes & Coplan, 2010). If we refer back to the description of some typical behaviors of shy children in the classroom (e.g., not volunteering to speak, avoiding eye contact, watching but not joining other children), it is easy to see how these behaviors seem as though a child is unengaged. In fact, this is very likely to be the case! However, this behavior has consequences. By denying themselves opportunities to directly participate in classroom activities with teachers and peers, shy children are also reducing the quality of their educational experiences.

Attention!

One reason why shy children may be less engaged in classroom activities is because they are not paying attention. For children with ADHD and other deficits of attention, it is the multiple distractions from the outside (e.g., noises in the hall) that keep them from focusing on instruction. As illustrated in the case study at the start of this chapter, for shy children, these multiple distractions are more likely to come from the *inside*. This may include nervousness about being called upon, worries about peer experiences at recess, or other anxieties about social or evaluative situations that interfere with shy children's ability to engage in classroom instruction. Discomfort in the classroom setting can undermine a child's ability to fully engage in the academic experience. This can occur during a class discussion, giving a presentation, interacting with peers, answering a direct question from the teacher, or during some other experience that is stressful for shy children. And when individuals feel threatened or fearful, their attention moves from the important academic tasks at hand to the perceived dangers in the environment.

Because the worry and anxiety common for shy children in classroom settings can distract them from attending to learning tasks, children who are shy *and* inattentive may be particularly at risk for academic difficulties. Indeed, research shows that being shy and inattentive can actually be more problematic for academic performance than being disruptive (Finn, Pannozzo, & Voelkl, 1995)! Children who are both shy and inattentive may not process course material as quickly as their less shy or more attentive peers, and because they are also likely to avoid asking for help from the teacher, their academic difficulties may persist and worsen. Remember how the squeaky wheel gets the grease? Disruptive children who are inattentive still tend to get what they need in terms of teacher assistance. Shy children, on the other hand, are unlikely to speak up when they don't understand,

and they're unlikely to understand if they have been too overwhelmed with worry to pay attention. Thus, they may continue to feel confused, and this may cause them to withdraw in the classroom even more.

However, just as poor attention skills may be particularly problematic for shy children, good attention skills may also be protective. Children with strong attention networks in place are able to retain focus even in the face of extreme stress. This may even be a way to cope with worry that stems from stressors in the classroom. For example, a shy child entering a new social environment could make use of a high ability to attend by carefully and efficiently watching a group of children interact. This would help such a child to determine relatively quickly how to join the group in a way that feels safe and comfortable.

Children with superior attention skills also tend to have good social skills, which may also be particularly helpful for shy children. For example, one of our studies with early elementary aged children demonstrated that shyer children who were more attentive were rated higher in social competence (Rudasill & Konold, 2008). In this case, attention was protective for children who were shy, possibly giving them the resources to overcome their reticence or worry in unfamiliar or stressful situations. Moreover, in a series of studies, researcher Nathan Fox and his colleagues (Degnan & Fox, 2007; White, McDermott, Degnan, Henderson, & Fox, 2011) have shown that the ability to attend (specifically to *shift* attention) decreases the likelihood that shy young children will go on to develop problems with anxiety. It is speculated that these attentive abilities allow shy children to more easily move their attention away from potential sources of stress. Applied to academic outcomes, it seems that strong attention enables shy children to shift their attention to what is required by the situation (e.g., teacher instruction) and away from distracting stimuli (e.g., internal messages of stress and worry, evaluation, or social concerns), resulting in better academic engagement and, ultimately, success.

Testing, Testing!

Another factor to consider in the underperformance of shy children is the nature of the testing situations that they are often faced with (Crozier & Perkins, 2002). Although formal tests do not comprise the only type of academic assessment, they remain common in elementary classrooms. The evaluative and high-stress nature of testing conditions makes such situations likely to produce anxiety and poor performance among shy children. Shy children's discomfort in a testing situation is illustrated in a study of 1st-graders in Finland by Rikka Hirvonen and her colleagues (Hirvonen, Aunola, Alatupa, Viljaranta, & Nurmi, 2013). Children with higher levels of shyness were more likely to show anxiety and helplessness during testing sessions than their classmates who were not as shy.

The effects of testing situations on shy children's performance appear to be related to age. Among younger children, concern about evaluation primarily affects speech. Thus, performance during tests requiring expressive speech (e.g., vocabulary knowledge) is most likely to suffer. In this regard, when shy children are required to read aloud (to the class, to the teacher, or to a small group), name objects, or tell a story (recall our description of show-and-tell), they will probably not provide an accurate picture of their ability or knowledge. When children get older, fear of evaluation often extends to more processes, such as the ability to solve a problem, write a paragraph, or shoot a basketball. Thus, although shy children's speech may be less affected, their desire to blend in with the crowd may be amplified, and their performance across a wider range of tasks can be affected.

There is also some evidence to suggest that the context and type of testing may also play a role. In a fascinating study, researchers Ray Crozier and Kristen Hostettler (2003) tested shy and non-shy children's math and verbal abilities under three conditions: (1) one-on-one with verbal responses; (2) one-on-one with written responses; and (3) group testing with written responses. Although we might have speculated that shy children would have performed worse in the group setting (because of the social nature of the group), they performed just as well as the non-shy children in this context. Instead, shy children performed worse than their non-shy classmates when tested one-on-one with an adult examiner. This was true even when they did not have to verbalize their responses.

Crozier and Hostettler suggest that shy children's dislike of social evaluation and being the center of attention was distracting to the extent that it hindered their ability to perform well on assessments where they were, indeed, the center of attention. This appeared to apply even when someone was simply watching them write their answers. More research is required to better understand how shy children might react to different testing circumstances. However, this is certainly something for teachers to keep in mind in their own classrooms.

Talking the Talk

The final factor we consider in the academic achievement of shy children relates specifically to their language skills. "Talking less" is a defining feature of shyness. However, shy children have also been consistently demonstrated to perform worse on standardized tests of language and verbal skills, starting as early as preschool. It is likely that shy children's poorer academic performance overall is influenced by their language and verbal skills.

We have put forth several theories to account for why shy children perform worse on tests of language (Coplan & Evans, 2009)—and they may also apply to different extents to our broader discussion of shyness and overall academic performance. The first we call *a lack of practice results in a lack of perfect.* This is similar to something we discussed in Chapter 4 about social skills. Because they are anxious around peers and concerned about social evaluation, shy children have fewer speaking experiences. This means that they also have fewer opportunities to practice and develop their language skills. Over time, this can lead to an actual deficit in language ability. This simple proposition certainly makes a lot of sense; all of us can relate to the notion that skill in any area improves with practice!

A second suggestion we call *I know it but I won't say it.* That is, shy children may not actually lag behind their less-shy peers in language knowledge, but they are unable to demonstrate this knowledge when called upon to do so, such as in a formal assessments where speaking in front of an examiner is required. This is related to our earlier discussion of the stresses of different testing situations for shy children. Shy children tend to feel anxious when they are being evaluated, and this reduces their ability to perform to the best of their ability. This re-emphasizes a key theme of this chapter for teachers to keep in mind. Shy children may be hindered by a performance deficit that is not necessarily reflective of a competence deficit.

The third theory we call *a bird in the hand is worth two in the bush.* The idea here is that shy children tend to play it safe in all aspects of life, and particularly in the social realm. Thus, if they are less likely to take risks, they may also be more inclined to leave a test item blank, for example, than hazard a guess that could be incorrect. The foundation of this theory is a common thread across shy children's behaviors: the known is preferred to the unknown. The final idea is called *bold is better.* This theory pulls back from shy children and refocuses on bold children. Here, the idea is that being very socially outgoing may afford a significant language *advantage.* This is quite plausible and consistent with the first theory about *practice makes perfect.* Children who practice language frequently should excel in this area. With this in mind, it may not be that shy children are *worse,* per se, at language, but that the bold children we are comparing them to tend to be better. This would seem to apply to the broader context of the classroom as well. Bold and talkative children may particularly excel, rendering shy children less impressive by comparison.

POSITIVE ASPECTS OF SHYNESS IN THE CLASSROOM

We have seen that the general nature of classroom settings has implications for shy children's academic and social behavior. Academically, shy children tend to perform less well than their non-shy peers, particularly on assessments of language that require speaking, and are prone to heightened performance anxiety that hinders their abilities to demonstrate what they know. They do not like being the center of attention, and will likely feel uncomfortable when they are being singled out, even for positive reasons (e.g., praised in front of the class for answering a question correctly). They also tend to appear less engaged in classroom activities, are generally reluctant to volunteer or initiate interactions with teachers and sometimes peers, and potentially receive less of a "dose" of instruction because of their reticence in classroom contexts. Thus, it is the combination of the social and evaluative aspects of the classroom environment, as well as unfamiliarity and change, that make it a difficult space for shy children to navigate.

Having said that, it is important to reiterate a point we made in Chapter 4. Not all shy children have problems at school. Similarly, shy behavior is not always viewed negatively by teachers and in the classroom. For example, shy children are not disruptive to teacher instruction or classroom activities. Thus, although they are less inclined to receive teacher attention, they are also less inclined to have negative or punitive interactions with teachers. Because of their quiet style, teachers may tend to view shy children as "good kids" and conclude that they are well behaved. They are unlikely to get into trouble—shy children are rarely aggressive or have problematic conduct. Indeed, shy children appear to be self-regulated—they sit quietly, do not call out or disrupt class, and follow instructions—but shy children *are* often struggling to regulate their anxiety and worry. *Highly regulated* shy children are those that look teachers and peers in the eye during social interactions, speak up during classroom activities, engage socially with peers, and are able to overcome their social and evaluative concerns to function successfully in the classroom. Indeed, well-regulated shy children probably would not appear shy, and may not need your special attention!

To summarize, in this chapter, we have focused on the characteristics of the elementary classroom that make it a potentially stressful environment for shy children. Specifically, we noted the unfamiliarity and inherently social nature of the classroom environment that are difficult for shy children. We also discussed some typical behaviors of shy children in the classroom, and the specific effects on shy children's academic outcomes. In the next chapter we will focus on shy children and their teachers, with attention to how teachers view and interact with shy children and the types of relationships that they form.

CHAPTER 6

Shy Children and Teachers

CASE STUDY: NOT GETTING TO KNOW YOU

It was the first day of school and Sheila intended to learn the names of all of the students in her 5th-grade class by the end of the day. This is no easy feat, but experience had shown her that students respond well when she learned their names, and they feel extra special when she showed that she made it a high priority.

Mike walked into the classroom and found his seat. He was seated near the edge of the room, and once he sat down, he stayed there. He didn't interact with the other children much, nor did he talk to Sheila.

Sheila realized near the end of the day that she had hardly noticed Mike, nor had she learned his name. It took a concerted effort to learn Mike's name. On the other hand, the more boisterous students' names had come to Sheila almost immediately. She had even learned some other facts about several other students who were more talkative—they willingly shared information with her!

It was this experience that illustrated to Sheila how easy it is for a shy child to *fly under the radar*, and miss out on interactions with the teacher and other children in the classroom. Mike's first day of school was very different from most children's, yet this was typical for him in new environments.

Having spent much of this book so far discussing various aspects of shyness from the perspective of the child, in this chapter we change our focus to *teachers*. Given shy children's unique characteristics and associated behaviors, it should not be surprising that there is growing research to indicate that teachers think about, interact with, and develop relationships with shy children in ways that are different than for other types of students in their classes. In the following pages we discuss: (1) the critical role that teachers play in shy children's experiences at school; (2) teachers' attitudes, beliefs, and perceptions about shy children; (3) how teachers typically interact with shy children; and (4) the nature of the relationships that teachers might form with their shy students.

TEACHERS' INFLUENCES ON SHY CHILDREN

Teachers have a critically important role in fostering many aspects of children's development. A teacher is the primary adult in a child's life outside of the home, and plays a central role in not only nurturing a child's academic development, but the development of the *whole* child. Indeed, teachers are often described as acting *in loco parentis* (in the place of the parent). This is often true across many domains.

In Chapter 4's discussion of parenting, we spent some time reviewing the importance of attachment relationships. Recall that parents with secure attachment relationships with their children are more likely to provide a secure base from which their children explore their environments. Ideally, teachers can also serve in this capacity, allowing children to reap the benefits of exploring the classroom environment and beyond (more about this later). Also, like parents, teachers are *models* of behavior for children. When teachers model positive and adaptive behaviors, such as demonstrating prosocial interactions, this sends powerful messages to children about appropriate ways to initiate and respond to interactions with others. In this way, and many others, teachers are often described as enacting an *invisible hand* (see Box 6.1) in the classroom, establishing the social context in which children interact with one another.

In the case of *shy* children, teachers appear to be particularly influential for social, emotional, and academic success in the classroom in large part because they help to set the *emotional climate* of a classroom. The emotional

---

Box 6.1. THE INVISIBLE HAND

Teachers create the social milieu of the classroom in how they interact with children, as well as how they establish and reinforce the nature of interactions between children. In this regard, Thomas Farmer and colleagues (Farmer, Hamm, & Hamm, 2011) used the term *invisible hand* as a metaphor to describe how teachers guide the development of children's peer relationships in the classroom.

Teachers who speak calmly to children, encourage prosocial interactions between children, monitor children's interactions with each other, and use preventive classroom management techniques are actively creating a positive social environment in the classroom. Such environments provide shy children (and other children) optimal settings for practicing social skills and developing friendships. This is particularly important for shy children. As we discussed in Chapter 4, shy children struggle in social relationships, so the role of teachers in the development of social skills cannot be overstated.

climate of a classroom is the feeling of warmth and support shared between teachers and students. In a classroom with a positive emotional climate, there will be smiling, laughter, positive conversational tone, respectful language, and consideration or awareness of the needs of all children. Teachers are warm and responsive to children's needs, as well as sensitive to children's perspectives.

Because of their sensitivity to novelty and their distress in evaluative or social situations, shy children seem to be particularly susceptible to the influence of classroom climate. That is, compared to their more outgoing classmates, shy children are more sensitive to both the benefits of an emotionally warm and supportive classroom climate, as well as the downsides of a more aversive and unsupportive climate. Teachers who create a positive emotional classroom climate signal to shy children that the classroom is an accepting environment where they will be treated fairly and not harshly evaluated. Of course, these qualities are beneficial for all children, but appear to pay particularly big dividends for shy children. Indeed, for shy students, such a classroom may make the difference between engaging productively in class and shutting down.

Shy children tend to warm up more easily and are generally put at ease in classrooms where teachers are kind and understanding. Indeed, such behaviors can immediately combat shy children's fear of evaluation because they send the message that children are accepted even if they fail or make mistakes, and promote the teachers' role as a secure base. (Remember that one of the fears shy children typically bring with them to school is that they will be negatively evaluated by their teacher). In this same vein, teachers' role as models for children's social behavior in the classroom also influences the development of classroom climate. For example, teachers who engage in positive interactions with children and monitor children's interactions with one another are more likely to establish a tone for the social environment of the classroom that is inviting for shy children who are insecure and anxious in social situations.

Research results have borne this out. For example, in a study of 1st-graders, we found that shy children who were in classrooms with highly sensitive teachers were more likely to be actively engaged in classroom activities than shy children in classrooms with teachers who were lower in sensitivity (Buhs, Rudasill, Kalutskaya, & Griese, 2015). Similarly, researcher Heidi Gazelle (2006) found that shy 1st-graders were particularly prone to be rejected by peers in classrooms with lower levels of emotionally supportive climates. In contrast, in classrooms with more positive and supportive climates, shy children were considerably less likely to experience such peer difficulties. In a follow-up study, Gazelle and her colleagues (Spangler Avant, Gazelle, & Faldowski, 2011) further demonstrated that although shy elementary school children were more likely than their more social peers to experience peer exclusion in the first few months of the school year, in classrooms with more positive emotional climates, this was no longer the case by the end of the school year.

Classrooms with less positive or more negative emotional climates are marked by harsher and less sensitive teacher behaviors, negative teacher-child interactions, and low regard for children's needs. Teachers who have stricter, more rigid, or more distant ways of interacting in the classroom may be inadvertently sending messages to shy students that reinforce these children's heightened feelings of fear of being negatively evaluated. Such negative teacher conduct also fails to establish an appropriate model of behavior for students to emulate in their interactions with one another, which in turn may worsen negative experiences with classmates for shy children. As a result, shy children are more likely to be withdrawn and quiet in such insensitive and nonresponsive classroom environments, as their fears, self-consciousness, and insecurities are not well understood, and their needs remain largely unmet.

Even when teachers are warm and accepting, model and strive to create positive social interactions in the classroom, and endeavor to make their classrooms welcoming to all of their students, they *still* may miss the needs of their shy students if they are not attuned to them. As we discussed in Chapter 5, shyness can be experienced mostly *inside* (particularly among older children), and shy children often behave and respond in the classroom in ways that make them less likely to be noticed by teachers. Thus, a teacher's ability to meet the needs of his or her shy students depends in large part on awareness of the behaviors and unique needs of shy children.

In this regard, teachers who anticipate the extraordinary stress often felt by shy children at the start of the school year will be more likely to put safeguards into place to facilitate this transition. For example, teachers of younger children might arrange to meet with parents prior to the beginning of the year to help identify which children might be shy and benefit from some additional emotional and instrumental support. Alternatively, the teacher may engage in careful observations during the first several activities of the school day, with an eye toward identifying particularly shy children. Whatever the case, a more sensitive and responsive teacher of younger children would seek to deliberately establish a social situation in the classroom that is less stressful and uncertain not only for shy children, but for all children. This could involve partnering shy children with friendly and outgoing peers, or having highly structured activities where there is little to no uncertainty involved (see Chapter 8 for our extensive discussion of strategies to help shy children in the classroom).

For older shy children, where social evaluative concerns may be greater, teachers who are especially tuned in will be likely to recognize the discomfort shy children have in being singled out and the center of attention. For example, a teacher with sensitivity regarding shy children's worries will minimize the number of instances where students need to introduce themselves to the class or perform in front of a group of new or relatively unfamiliar peers (and an unfamiliar teacher). This teacher will also structure classroom activities so that there is little uncertainty in peer interactions (who sits with whom, what role each student has), thus reducing the early fears regarding navigating the deeply social demands of the classroom environment.

TEACHERS' VIEWS ABOUT SHY CHILDREN

CASE STUDY: NOT RIGHT TO REMAIN SILENT

Amy is a 2nd-grade student whose shyness is evident only in certain situations. For example, among her familiar classmates and friends, Amy is comfortable and often even outgoing.

However, with adults, particularly those who seem less warm and more distant, Amy's behavior often appears to be quite shy. In these contexts, Amy is very reluctant to initiate interactions, tends to keep quiet even when she is confused about a lesson or topic, and is often too intimidated to respond even when she is engaged directly.

One day, Amy was working at her table and a classmate asked to borrow her pencil. After she tossed the pencil to him, the student immediately told the teacher that Amy had just thrown a pencil at him. When the teacher asked what happened, Amy just looked at her feet and did not answer. The teacher took this to mean that Amy was, indeed, guilty of throwing the pencil at this student. Amy felt intimidated by her teacher—too intimidated to speak up in her defense.

Because the teacher did not recognize Amy's behavior as shyness, she mistook Amy's withdrawn behavior as guilt, rather than fear.

There is widespread agreement among educators that optimal classrooms are those in which teachers *get to know* the children in their charge. Familiarity and better understanding allows teachers to best meet the specific needs of their different students. This is a laudable goal, and highly important for successful learning. Indeed, when teachers get to know the children in their classes, they are better able to help students capitalize on their strengths, feel connected to school, and be motivated to work hard. As we have just seen, this is particularly important for teachers of shy students. In this regard, identifying and understanding the characteristics of shy children is instrumental for helping them more easily adjust to the classroom environment.

As illustrated in the case study that led off this section, a better understanding of the motivations behind Amy's shy behaviors, particularly around adults, would have been very helpful to the teacher as she worked with Amy in this scenario. However, a defining feature of shy children is that they are quiet, thus making it more difficult for teachers to get to know them, particularly compared to more talkative and forthcoming students. Recall the case study from the beginning of the chapter. The teacher, Sheila, worked hard to get to know her students' names on the first day of school, and even learned several other facts about some of her students by the end of the day. However, *she hadn't even learned the shy child Mike's name.*

So, whereas more boisterous students are much more likely to make themselves readily apparent to teachers, initiate interactions with them, and offer information willingly, shy children are much more likely to be reserved, especially at the beginning of the year when the teacher and classroom are new. As we have seen, even as the school year progresses, shy children often remain uncomfortable in the classroom, which continues to hinder the establishment of a positive rapport with teachers. This quiet style may make it more difficult for teachers to engage shy children in conversations. As well, shy children's tendency to withdraw means there is less opportunity to observe their interactions with peers. Also, teachers expect children to participate by asking questions and volunteering answers in class, but shy children are typically reluctant to do so. Collectively, then, shy children's behavior in the classroom makes it difficult for their teachers to get to know them and understand the role shyness is having in their school experiences. This results in teacher perceptions of shy children that tend to be inaccurate and often overly negative.

Engagement

Because of shy children's quiet style and general reticence to actively participate in all aspects of the classroom, it is not surprising that teachers more often develop negative perceptions of their interest, engagement, and preparation. Shy children may appear uninterested, unprepared, or unable to participate in class activities. This is particularly likely to occur during class activities involving group instruction, when children are asked to speak in front of the class, or when children have to problem-solve with a group of peers. As we have discussed previously, shy children tend to stay quiet during class discussions and wait for their more boisterous and outgoing peers to speak up. The good news is that there is growing evidence to suggest that teachers are becoming increasingly aware of the potential problems that may be experienced by shy children (Bosacki, Coplan, Rose-Krasnor, & Hughes, 2011). For example, in one of our recent studies, teachers of young children indicated that they would be just as worried about shy children in their classes as they would be about physically aggressive children (Coplan, Bullock, Archbell, & Bosacki, 2015). However, there is some potentially bad news to go along with this. As we have just seen, teachers tend to ascribe more negative attributes to children who display shy behaviors in their classes.

There are other problems, too. Our research and experience in class-rooms suggests that teachers may view shy children as uninterested in class-room material or unprepared for class activities. Let's consider an example of how this might unfold. A shy child looks down at his desk while the teacher is delivering instruction, whereas other children are looking up, making eye contact, smiling, and/or giving other visual cues that they are paying attention. Although the shy child is looking down because of social anxiety and fear of being noticed by the teacher or classmates, this behavior appears to the teacher as a lack of interest, or possibly disrespect. Similarly, when shy children fail to raise their hands to volunteer answers during class discussion, or seem reluctant to answer direct teacher questions, they may come across as unprepared rather than fearful.

Consider another possible classroom-based scenario. The teacher has assigned 4th-grade students book report presentations. The students have 3 weeks to complete the assignment, so there is ample time to read a book and prepare a report. On the day of the presentations, though, a student who is very shy refuses to give his book report. Although he fears negative evalua-tion by the teacher, he is *more* fearful of having his peers stare at him and of being the center of attention. He does not tell the teacher anything about his inner turmoil (talking to the teacher about this is also too intimidating), he just refuses to give the book report. As a result, his teacher could conclude that he is lazy or does not care about his schoolwork. It is not difficult to see how a shy child's behavior may be misconstrued.

Academic Abilities

It has long been suggested that teachers can be prone to making inferences related to students' academic abilities based on their perceptions of the stu-dents' verbal and social behaviors. For example, in a 1967 study of kin-dergarten teachers, Edward Gordon and Alexander Thomas found that teachers rated more prosocial students (e.g., those who appeared to lead group activities) as being more intelligent than their less sociable classmates. Thus, shy children's refusal or hesitance to speak up may be construed by teachers as a lack of ability, rather than as stemming from social withdraw-al or fear. Remember our discussion from Chapter 5 of show-and-tell and how that activity presents the perfect combination of all major stresses ex-perienced by shy children? Because shy children tend to be quiet and less behaviorally engaged in classroom activities, teachers tend to underestimate their abilities.

However, as illustrated in some of our recent research, there is more to it than just teachers thinking that shy children might not do as well ac-ademically in their class as compared to more outgoing students. In one study (Coplan, Hughes, Bosacki, & Rose-Krasnor, 2011), we presented elementary school teachers with vignettes depicting hypothetical children displaying shy/quiet, exuberant/talkative, and average/typical behaviors in the classroom. After each vignette, teachers responded to follow-up questions assessing their attitudes and beliefs about each hypothetical child. Overall, teachers reported that shy children would not only be likely to do more poorly academically but also that they were less intelligent than their average and more talkative classmates. We found similar results with preservice teachers (i.e., university students in a Bachelor of Education Program) using vignettes of hypothetical shy/quiet, exuberant/talkative, and average/ typical behaviors in the classroom (Deng, Trainin, Rudasill, Kalutskaya, Wessels, Torquati, & Coplan, 2015). These teachers-in-training also perceived hypothetical shy children as less likely to be academically successful than exuberant and typical children.

This finding does not bode particularly well for shy children's academic success in the classroom. Teachers' perceptions regarding students' intelligence and academic skills can lead to the creation of a self-fulfilling prophecy. That is, if shy students are initially not expected to do well academically, over time their actual academic performance may *live down* to these expectations.

Consistent with this idea, in studies we have conducted with elementary-aged children, results have suggested that children's shyness is linked to teacher perceptions of their academic achievement, but *not* standardized assessments of their achievement (Hughes & Coplan, 2010). This is an important point, because it suggests that shy children's academic achievement deficits may be more about teachers' *perceptions* of children's ability than actual ability. So keeping in mind the potential for teachers to misconstrue quiet children's capabilities may be important for offsetting a self-fulfilling prophecy.

Interestingly, some teacher attitudes and beliefs about shy students appear to be influenced by their *own* shyness. In the study of elementary teachers we just described (Coplan et al., 2011), we also found that, although all teachers tended to agree that shy children would experience academic difficulties in class, non-shy teachers appeared to attribute these difficulties to lower child intelligence, whereas shy teachers did not. It seems likely that shy teachers' own experiences with shyness fostered their beliefs that shy children's academic difficulties are often due to other factors (anxiety, self-consciousness). This too may not bode well for shy students, given research by Lauren Decker and Sara Rimm-Kaufman (2008), who found that individuals choosing to enter the teaching profession are more likely to be extroverted as compared to the general population. As such, shy children are most likely to encounter teachers who are less shy than themselves, and thus less likely to be aware of and sensitive to the different needs that shy children may have.

TEACHERS' INTERACTIONS WITH SHY CHILDREN

Historically, shy children have often been described as being mostly ignored by teachers. Some researchers even suggested that educators may encourage shyness among students because such behaviors help to maintain order in the classroom. Notwithstanding, shy children likely receive less teacher attention than bolder students because they are not disruptive, boisterous, or demanding. This lack of attention may also be compounded as children progress through school. For example, in early childhood settings, such as preschool, we have found that teachers tend to notice shy children's quiet style and make efforts to draw them out (Coplan & Prakash, 2003). The emphasis in early childhood classrooms on one-on-one interactions with teachers and play-based activities lends itself nicely to this kind of teacher attention for children who are withdrawn in their social behavior.

However, increased curricular demands on teachers and less time with students can often result in even less attention being paid to shy, quiet, and unobtrusive children. As children move into elementary grades, the academic press that pervades the environment makes it more difficult for teachers to take time out from the delivery of instruction for children who do not seem disruptive or problematic (i.e., shy children). Our research suggests that the constant press on teachers in elementary classrooms to meet daily demands (classroom management, instructional requirements, administrative duties) means that teachers may not always have the awareness or time necessary to intervene, particularly with children who are not causing disruption to classroom activities (Rudasill & Rimm-Kaufman, 2009; Rudasill, 2011).

As a result, shy children receive a smaller *dose* of instruction and less interaction from their teachers. Our research shows that shy children initiate and receive fewer interactions with teachers than their peers who are less shy, and their peers who are less regulated (Rudasill & Rimm-Kaufman, 2009). Other research by Jeremy Finn and colleagues (Finn et al., 1995) revealed that being withdrawn in class (and going unnoticed by teachers) put children more at-risk for academic difficulties than being disruptive, and that this is likely due to the fact that disruptive children receive far more teacher attention than do shy and withdrawn children. Although negative attention is less than ideal, it may be better than no attention at all when it comes to meeting children's needs and facilitating their academic success.

It is not hard to explain why teachers might pay more attention to outgoing, boisterous, and disruptive students. A teacher's intervention with such children is necessitated by the pressing need to provide a safe and learning-conducive environment in the classroom (a need supported by continual pressure on the teacher by the administration and parents). In contrast, a teacher's tendency to intervene with a shy child in an elementary classroom requires not only an understanding of shy children's (largely internal) characteristics, but also an acknowledgment of ways that the school and classroom environment may be particularly stressful for such a child. In this way, it is easy for shy children to slip through the cracks. They behave in a manner that is convenient for most teachers already; such behavior is not disruptive to the delivery of instruction and may even be a much-needed relief to a new and overwhelmed teacher!

TEACHERS' RELATIONSHIPS WITH SHY CHILDREN

In the final section of this chapter, we take a closer look at the relationships that teachers may form with their shy students. The combination of shy children's tendency to withdraw from social interactions and their fear of social evaluation by teachers often results in difficulty forming relationships with teachers. Teacher-child relationships are rooted in the notion of parent-child attachment relationships (see Chapter 4). Recall that a secure attachment relationship between a parent and child reflects a child's belief that the parent is a safe and reliable caregiver. From this positive relationship, the child typically develops a more optimistic view of the world and his or her place in it.

As children move to the school context, teachers become important adults in their lives, and the teacher-child relationship can become another attachment-type relationship. Although not a replacement for parents, teachers are able to provide a powerful sense of support and safety, giving children the freedom to take risks and to grow in a nurturing environment (Pianta, 1999). Thus, positive or high-quality teacher-child relationships (e.g., characterized by higher levels of closeness and lower levels of conflict between teachers and children) have been consistently shown to be important for all children's academic and social success during the elementary years and beyond. For example, researchers Bridget Hamre and Robert Pianta (2001) found that more positive teacher-child relationships in kindergarten predicted greater social and academic success for children through grade 8.

Most relevant for us, high-quality relationships not only predict positive downstream success for children, they are also protective against risk when children are vulnerable. For example, high levels of teacher-child closeness, warmth, and mutual positive regard between the child and teacher have been shown to be protective for children who are at risk due to difficulties associated with poverty or behavior problems. On the other hand, high levels of conflict, marked by adversity and struggle, are predictive of such children's later academic, social, and behavioral difficulties. We have found a similar pattern for shy children. Our research has shown that high-quality teacher-child relationships can be protective for shy children, buffering them from difficulties with peer relationships and negative feelings about school (Arbeau, Coplan, & Weeks, 2010). Shy children, though, tend to have relationships with teachers that are neither close nor conflictual. That is, *they seem to struggle with developing any type of relationship with their teachers.* The fact that shy children are unlikely to form relationships with teachers is striking and underscores a previous point we made about how shy children tend to go unnoticed in the classroom.

It should be noted that there is some evidence to suggest that young shy children may be prone to developing *dependent* teacher-child relationships. Dependency is characterized by clinginess and overly needy behavior; children may insist on being with the teacher all the time, follow the teacher around, and ask excessive numbers of questions. Clearly this behavior would not apply to a child who has a fear of being negatively evaluated by the teacher, which may be why it appears only in young children when social evaluation is less salient. Sara Swenson (2015) conducted a study of preschool teachers' perceptions of their interactions with shy children in their classrooms, and she found that teachers consistently identified shy children as overly clingy.

We have found in our research that shy preschool children with more complex language skills were also more likely to have dependent relationships with their teachers (Rudasill, Rimm-Kaufman, Justice, & Pence, 2006). Although such teacher-child relationships are negative, as teachers perceive children who are dependent as requiring a lot of unnecessary attention, this negative relationship may be protective because teachers are interacting with the shy child. At the same time, we know that parenting that encourages clingy and needy behavior cultivates children's dependency and fear; it is likely that the same pitfalls would occur with dependent teacher-child relationships as well. Although it is not entirely clear how these early potentially dependent teacher-child relationships affect shy children's later school experiences, we do know that early relationships lay the groundwork for later teacher-child relationships and children's broader perceptions of the school experience.

So, we know that shy children have difficulty forming relationships with their teachers, especially positive or close relationships, yet shy children who have close relationships with their teachers appear to have better outcomes than shy children who do not. This appears to be particularly evident in the early years of elementary school, when children's educational groundwork is being established. Children who have positive experiences with teachers, including close relationships with teachers, have a firm foundation from which to successfully go forth into *other* school experiences that may be intimidating due to their novelty, such as the start of a new school year, or socially stressful, such as giving a presentation to the class. Thus, setting out to develop positive relationships with shy children is a promising point of intervention that teachers can use in their classrooms. We discuss this further in Chapter 8.

CONCLUSIONS

Teachers play a critical role in shaping the experiences shy children have in school. Best practices such as providing a supportive and positive classroom climate, engaging and interacting with students, and striving to forge positive relationships with students are especially important for putting shy children at ease in the classroom. As we conclude this chapter on shy children and their teachers, we also close this section of the book that is focused on describing shy children's experiences in the educational context. We move now to the last, and more practical, section of this book. In this last section, we will focus on *best practices* for teachers to assist shy children. This includes *general* strategies for helping shy children deal with anxiety and fear (Chapter 7), and then *specific* strategies for helping shy children be successful in the classroom (Chapter 8).

CHAPTER 7

Best Practices for Assisting Shy Children

Part I: General Approaches

CASE STUDY: REVISITING THE SWIMMING POOL

Once upon a time, a third mother also tried to teach her child how to swim. Upon arrival at the swimming pool for the first lesson—her child also said "I am too scared to go in the water!" and started to cry.

Unlike the first mother, who got angry and pushed too hard, or the second mother, who was worried and did not push hard enough, the third mother took a different approach. She said to her child, "I can see that you are scared—and that's okay. Let's start by taking a deep breath together. This can help us feel less scared. Good! Now, sometimes, even when you are feeling scared about something, we still need to try our best, and just do it one small step at a time."

So, that first day, the mother and the child did not even change into their bathing suits. Instead, they sat at the side of the pool together and watched the other children swim. The next time they came to the pool, they changed into their bathing suits, sat on the side of the pool again, but this time, they also dipped their toes in the water. The time after that, they dipped their legs in the pool up to their knees. The time after that, they sat on the first stair entering the pool, and then the next time they sat on the second stair, and so on with each subsequent visit. At each stage, the mother offered lots of support and encouragement. After several visits, the child went into the water on her own and was on her way to learning how to swim.

The moral of this story is a familiar one. For shy children in particular, *slow and steady wins the race.*

We have now reached the point in this book where we begin to consider practical applications that all of the background knowledge and previous research about shyness has taught us. In this chapter, we will focus on general techniques derived from developmental and clinical psychology that can be applied to assist shy children at school. These are broad approaches that can be used effectively across a wide range of contexts and circumstances (in the next chapter we review more specific best techniques). In the case study, we revisit the *learning to swim* scenario first introduced in Chapter 3, when we talked about parenting. The third mother described here had more success in getting her child to swim, employing various strategies derived from psychology that have been demonstrated to be particularly effective with shy and anxious children (e.g., emotion-focused parenting, relaxation, positive reinforcement, and graduated exposure). We will discuss each of these in detail in this chapter.

One important point that we would like to emphasize from the outset relates to *expectations* about change in shy children. As we have frequently emphasized in our discussions with parents of shy children, real change takes time—and there will be lots of ups and downs along the way. In our opinion, many people have unrealistic expectations about how much and how quickly shy children's behaviors can be altered at school. A few years ago, we conducted a review of how shy characters were depicted in storybooks for young children (Coplan, Hughes, & Rowsell, 2010). The idea here was that parents might be more likely to read their shy child a storybook that focused on a shy character. The manner in which this shy character was described and portrayed provides one way that mothers and children might come to form expectations about shyness.

In the 20 storybooks that we reviewed, we were quite pleased to find that authors presented surprisingly accurate representations of shyness across many domains. For example, the majority of the books referred to shyness as having a biological basis (e.g., "born that way"), as most likely to be evoked by new social situations or being the center of attention, and as having negative implications for children's peer experiences (e.g., getting teased at school) and well-being (e.g., low self-esteem, feelings of sadness). However, there was one area where the authors did not provide information that was consistent with research and theory about shyness. By the end of the storybooks, almost all of the shy characters (90%) had undergone a notable *change*, most often in the form of becoming less shy (e.g., "became more comfortable," "stopped blushing, "became brave enough," "found the courage to talk"). Although it is certainly understandable that most storybooks for shy children might have a *happy ending*, the moral portrayed in these books was that almost all shy children can change in a relatively short period of time. Moreover, these books suggest that a happy ending means *not* being shy. We think it is ultimately more helpful for parents and teachers to temper their expectations in this regard, and view their efforts to assist shy children as more of a longer-term project and from the perspective that shyness is a characteristic to *work with* rather than to change. With that in mind, we consider several general approaches that can be integrated into teachers' day-to-day interactions with shy children.

WITH A LITTLE HELP FROM MY FRIENDS?

As we have learned, much of shy children's challenges center around the peer group. Indeed, some of the primary reasons we potentially worry about shy children include their relative lack of peer interaction (and all the *good stuff* they might be missing out on as a result, as described in Chapter 4) and the negative experiences that they might encounter (e.g., exclusion, victimization) when they inevitably encounter peers at school. For these reasons (and many others), primary goals of intervention for shy children are to increase both the *quantity* (frequency) and *quality* of their peer interactions. With this in mind, it should not be surprising that our first recommendation for general approaches to intervention with shy children is to *involve other children*.

This is certainly not a new idea. As you may recall from Chapter 1, one of the first intervention programs specifically designed for shy children (conducted by researchers Lowenstein and Svendsen in 1938) consisted of *play therapy* with other shy and socially withdrawn peers. The goal of approaches like this is to provide a specifically tailored context where shy children are more likely to have success in their social interactions. The hope is that the mastery experiences and confidence that shy children might garner from interacting with other children in these settings will generalize to their social encounters at school.

Variations on this approach have met with some success in improving rates of social interaction among shy children. For example, Wyndol Furman and his colleagues (Furman, Rahe, & Hartup, 1979) conducted an intervention where shy preschoolers interacted with *younger* children, suggesting that shy children could benefit from having the (presumably novel) experience of being the more skilled partner during play. Using a somewhat different model, John Fantuzzo and his colleagues (Fantuzzo, Stovall, Schachtel, Goins, & Hal, 1987) trained more *sociable* children to make competent social initiations to shy peers as a means of encouraging more positive social experiences. Similarly, Jeanette Christopher and her colleagues trained classmates to serve as *peer helpers* for shy children (Christopher, Hansen, & MacMillan, 1991). In these studies, it was assumed that interacting and being assisted by more socially skilled and friendly children would facilitate social exchanges for shy children.

Given that shy children may also have deficits in social competence, direct instruction in social skills can also be effective in increasing peer interaction. Such *social skills training* programs are designed to teach children abilities that will facilitate competent social interactions. For example, we have recently developed the *Play Skills* program for shy preschoolers (Coplan, Schneider, Matheson, & Graham, 2010), which focuses on the acquisition and implementation of specific social strategies and techniques that are relevant for the challenges that they typically face (e.g., making eye contact, speaking during show-and-tell, inviting someone to play). In a series of weekly sessions, trained leaders help small groups of shy children to learn these skills during short circle time sessions. The children then practice and implement these skills during free play, facilitated by the group leaders. In two recent studies (Coplan et al., 2010; Chronis-Tuscano et al., 2015), we have shown that shy children who participated in the intervention demonstrated greater increases in peer interaction at school and greater reductions in anxiety as compared to a matched group of shy children who had yet to take part in the intervention.

Given that classrooms are full of students, teachers can easily incorporate peer-mediated approaches to interventions for shy children. Teachers should maintain overall goals of increasing the frequency and quality of shy children's social exchanges with peers. As suggested by the research we just described, pairing shy children with carefully chosen classmates and helping children acquire and practice relevant social skills can facilitate these goals. For example, it may be possible for teachers to incorporate social-skills training during circle time or other daily activities, and to use strategies during free play or group discussions to model and reinforce social skills. In the next chapter, we will discuss in more detail some specific strategies and particular situations for utilizing peer-mediated approaches. As well, the other general techniques discussed subsequently in this chapter can all be used as tools to increase social interaction among shy children.

ONE SMALL STEP AT A TIME

One of the most common practices in clinical psychology (and many other domains) is *graduated exposure.* This protocol was illustrated in the swimming pool example (the case study) at the beginning of this chapter. Essentially, graduated exposure breaks down a desired goal (e.g., go into the swimming pool) into a series of more attainable smaller minigoals that gradually become more challenging (e.g., dip your toes in the water, sit on the first step of the pool, go in up to your waist, etc.). The child is provided with support and encouragement as she slowly and eventually makes her way through these minigoals down the steps). This approach can be applied to a wide range of goals across a wide range of situations and contexts.

In one of our groups for parents of shy children, a father once described an excellent application of graduated exposure that he used to help his young son with a challenging social task. Every Friday after school, this father would pick up his son and take him to buy a Popsicle at the corner store on the way home. This was a way to celebrate and reward the completion of another week of school. Needless to say, the child really liked getting these Popsicles! However, being quite shy, the child did not want to participate in the purchase of the Popsicles, because he was too intimidated to speak to the person behind the counter. The father told his son that if he wanted a Popsicle each week, he was going to have to start participating in the process of acquiring the Popsicles, at least to some degree. So, the two of them sat down together and created a *ladder* that depicted the different steps that the child would attempt each week as he worked toward becoming a more active participant in Popsicle acquisition.

The first week, all the child had to do was go into the store with his father and stand just inside the door as the father ordered and paid for the Popsicle. Each week, the child's tasks became a little more challenging. For example, in the second week, the child had to take an additional two small footsteps toward the counter from inside the door while the father still ordered and paid for the Popsicle. In subsequent weeks, the child eventually worked his way up to even more challenging steps, including joining his father at the counter, making eye contact with the vendor, pointing at the Popsicle he wanted to order, and ordering the Popsicle using words. After a few months, while his father waited outside, the child succeeded in entering the store alone and ordering and paying for the Popsicle himself!

Teachers are not likely able to implement such a detailed and extensive hierarchy of minigoals for individual students in their classes. However, this general approach can be extremely fruitful for helping shy children gradually *face their fears*. It is important to remember that each child will require differently spaced steps in their ladders, and will proceed with these steps at their own individual paces. As you become increasingly familiar with your students' particular strengths and needs, you will become more adept at constructing these ladders so that each student can begin to regularly experience success. In Box 7.1 on the next page, we provide some tips for developing successful graduated exposure tasks.

EMOTION COACHING

Another general approach for teachers to employ in their interactions with shy students is derived from research on how parents talk to and teach their children about emotions. For example, researchers John Gottman and Joan Declaire (1997) have described the advantages of using an *emotion-coaching* style. Parents who espouse this approach are aware of—and can comfortably talk about—their own and their children's emotions. In particular, emotion coaches acknowledge and value the experience of negative emotions as an opportunity for both intimacy and constructive learning.

Box 7.1. Helpful Hints for Creating Graduated Exposure Ladders

- Emphasize, reinforce, attend to, and reward even small positive social gains
- Make sure the first step of the ladder is quite tiny, so the child can experience success
- After each step, praise and don't immediately force the next step (e.g., if the child goes into the water, give praise and let the child get out, instead of praise followed immediately by "now put your head under")
- When appropriate, push the child to accomplish the next step, but do it *gently*
- Be prepared for and expect failures and setbacks (practice . . . practice . . . practice . . . will help over time)
- Don't be discouraged if the child has problems with the next step (keep trying!)
- Remember that this is a longer-term project you and the child are embarking on (i.e., you may not notice significant change for a while)

This was illustrated by the mother of the child learning to swim in the case study at the beginning of this chapter. For example, she acknowledged and helped the child label the emotion ("I see that you are scared—and that's okay"), offered guidance on how to regulate these negative feelings ("Let's start by taking a deep breath together. This can help us feel less scared") and set limits and expectations about how to behave when you experience this emotion ("Now, sometimes, even when we are feeling scared about something, we still need to try our best, and just do it one small step at a time").

The goal for an emotion-coaching parent is to teach children how to regulate their emotions, not take them away. In contrast, some parents tend to use an *emotion-dismissing* style. Emotion-dismissing parents are not comfortable talking about their own feelings or their children's feelings, and seek to minimize and shorten emotional displays ("stop crying," "there is nothing to be scared of," "grow up"). As compared to their emotion-dismissing counterparts, parents who employ an emotion-coaching approach have children who develop better emotion regulation skills and have higher self-esteem.

Teachers can widely apply emotion-focused approaches in their classrooms. For example, researcher Sandee McClowry (2014) uses the phrase *scaffold and stretch* to describe how teachers can support shy students in becoming more comfortable in situations that they view as threatening or anxiety-provoking in the classroom. Consistent with emotion coaching, teachers are encouraged to acknowledge children's fear and discomfort, and set expectations for next steps in the process of gradually changing behavior to overcome the fear (stretching), while providing warmth and support (scaffolding). In her book *Temperament-Based Elementary Classroom Management* (2014), McClowry provides this example of an optimal response to a shy child: "I know that you would prefer to first watch the other children rather than join in, so let me stand with you a few minutes until you feel ready to work with them" (p. 53). This statement (1) acknowledges the child's feelings of wariness around peers; (2) demonstrates support for the child; and (3) sets up the expectation that the shy child will join his peers in a few minutes. McClowry notes that such responses can be very positive and powerful because they communicate to children that the teacher understands their shyness and wants to help them be successful in the classroom.

CHALLENGING BAD THOUGHTS

Imagine you are out walking one afternoon and you happen to see your friend across a busy street. You wave to her and call out, but she just keeps walking and does not respond. Most people would react to this situation by thinking something like, "Hmmm, I guess she did not see me," and continue on with their day. However, people suffering from social anxiety disorder would likely have a much more negative reaction to this incident. Immediate thoughts that might flood into their heads would be something like, "Uh oh . . . she ignored me. She must be mad at me about something! What did I do? Oh no—I must have done something or said something wrong the last time we talked. She must be really mad. Now she is going to tell everyone what a bad person I am. This is going to be a real problem. What am I going to do?" A socially anxious person might then spend days ruminating and worrying about this, too nervous to actually contact this friend.

As illustrated by this example, negative thought patterns are key components of anxiety. The socially anxious individual characterized here is displaying some of the common *cognitive biases* that are known to perpetuate and worsen anxiety over time. These include tendencies to perceive threat, catastrophize (i.e., immediately expect the worst), and blame oneself for expected failures in social situations. Cognitive Behavioral Therapy (CBT) is a practice of replacing distorted and negative thought patterns and beliefs with realistic and adaptive ones. CBT is the most well-established, empirically supported, and often-used treatment for children and adults suffering from anxiety disorders (for comprehensive reviews, see Compton et al., 2004; Hofmann, Asnaani, Vonk, Sawyer, & Fang, 2012). A primary focus of this therapeutic technique is teaching anxious individuals concrete strategies for reducing negative thinking patterns.

Addressing negative thoughts provides another broad approach for teachers to consider when helping shy students in their classes. Clinical psychologists receive extensive and specific training to use CBT with clients. Thus, what we are suggesting here is that teachers should become aware that many shy children might be prone to these types of negative thoughts. For example, it would be helpful for teachers to consider that their neutral or ambiguous statements, gestures, or facial expressions might be interpreted as negative or threatening by shy students. Just as we've noted in other chapters, awareness of shy children's different ways of taking in information can be useful in understanding and helping them deal with their fears and worries.

MIND OVER MATTER

From a somewhat different perspective, *mindfulness*-based approaches arose from Buddhist meditation traditions where individuals are trained to attend to and focus on sensations, thoughts, and emotions as they are experienced (and *without judgment*). Contemporary mindfulness programs have been most influenced by the work of researcher Jon Kabat-Zinn (1990). The central goal of mindful practices is for individuals to become able to live more fully in the moment and, as such, be more open and accepting toward both negative and positive aspects of life. The primary mindfulness intervention used with children is *Mindfulness-Based Cognitive Therapy for Children* (MBCT-C). This approach to intervention has been receiving widespread and growing attention in recent years (Baer, 2014).

Mindfulness activities are centered on helping individuals recalibrate their experiences with the world so that they pay attention to all aspects (thoughts, emotions, physical sensations) of each experience, even if they are unpleasant. An example of an activity intended to bring about this awareness and attention is the raisin exercise, in which participants are given a raisin and are instructed to just observe the raisin as if it is completely novel to them. Then they are instructed to pick up the raisin, feel its texture, and notice its smell. Then they are told to taste the raisin and notice the sensations associated with the raisin as they eat it. This is mindfulness in eating, and it is meant to remind individuals that we spend much of our lives automatically carrying out activities without thinking about, appreciating, or truly experiencing them. Other mindfulness-related activities include body scan, sitting meditation, walking meditation, and mindful yoga—in all of these activities, individuals are instructed to pay attention to the activity as they are doing it (e.g., walking) including the associated thoughts, emotions, and sensations associated with that activity (e.g., the sensation of their feet touching the floor). The purpose of all of these activities is to train one's thinking to stay focused in the moment and to be open to the feelings and thoughts that come during that moment, even if they are negative or unpleasant. This teaches focus and attention, which can counteract the negative effects of anxiety and worry.

Mindfulness techniques that are adapted for younger participants take into account that children typically have less capacity for sitting still for long periods of time. Moreover, most mindfulness programs for children take advantage of the family and school support systems that can facilitate the intervention progress. Thus, typical mindfulness programs for children are about 8 weeks, and usually for only 90 minutes per week. The mindfulness exercises are often shorter and more repetitive to make them easier for children. In addition, these mindfulness programs can be easily implemented in the school environment, either in the classroom itself or in smaller group sessions. Parents may also be invited to participate in some of the sessions so that they can provide support at home, and teachers can facilitate communication between home and school about the program.

There is emerging evidence that mindfulness-based interventions are effective for helping children who are experiencing anxiety. In a recent meta-analysis summarizing findings from experimental studies on mindfulness for improving mental health in children and adolescents, Kannan Kallapiran and colleagues concluded that mindfulness-based interventions are at least as effective as cognitive behavior therapy approaches (Kallapiran, Koo, Kirubakaran, & Hancock, 2015). The principles of mindfulness, such as paying attention to your emotions, thoughts, and sensations in the moment, may be easily implemented in the classroom by teachers as reminders to students individually (for example, if students are or have been engaged in mindful practices) or to the class (reminders to "take a deep breath") to help students benefit from a momentary pause in the mad dash of the day's activities.

CLASSROOM-BASED PROGRAMS FOR SHY AND ANXIOUS CHILDREN

In this last section, we provide background information on some classroom-based intervention programs that have been developed to help shy, socially withdrawn, and anxious children at school. Teachers who are interested in these programs should consult the websites listed and the references cited.

FRIENDS for Life

The first program is *FRIENDS for Life*, which was developed by researcher Paula Barrett and colleagues (Shortt, Barrett, & Fox, 2001). This intervention program, based primarily on Cognitive Behavioral Therapy (CBT), can be delivered at school by teachers (who receive special training), integrated into the curriculum. The goal is to assist children in learning CBT skills and techniques that have been shown to help manage anxiety, such as relaxation, and challenging biased cognitions (e.g., turning "negative red thoughts" into "positive green thoughts"). The word FRIENDS is actually an acronym, created to help children and adolescents remember a series of steps that they can follow when they feel nervous, worrisome, or anxious (see Box 7.2).

The FRIENDS program has been widely adopted around the world. Results from several studies indicate that this program is effective in reducing anxiety (Rodgers & Dunsmuir, 2015). Indeed, in 2004, the World Health Organization cited FRIENDS for Life as the first evidence-based program deemed effective in reducing anxiety in children and adolescents (WHO Report on Prevention of Mental Disorders, 2004). More information about FRIENDS can be found at www.friendsrt.com/ and www.pathwayshrc.com.au/.

INSIGHTS into Children's Temperament

INSIGHTS into Children's Temperament is an intervention program developed by researcher Sandee McClowry (2014), referred to earlier in this chapter. INSIGHTS is a school-based intervention program that teaches social and emotional skills to children, with a particular sensitivity toward children with different temperaments. The purpose of the program is to help children and their teachers (and parents) understand temperament and how individual differences in children's temperament play a role in the ways that children respond to people and situations in their environments. INSIGHTS includes a classroom-based component where children learn about four different temperament *types* using puppets (including a socially withdrawn puppet named Coretta the Cautious). Similarly, there

---

Box 7.2. FRIENDS for Life

F—Feeling worried?

R—Relax and feel good

I—I can do it!

E—Explore solutions and coping step plans

N—Now reward yourself

D—Don't forget to practice

S—Stay cool!

is a teacher-training component focused on the temperament types where teachers see video vignettes of children dealing with various situations that may be challenging for the different temperaments. For example, Coretta may find having a substitute teacher particularly challenging. Once children and teachers are aware of the basic characteristics and the challenges of each of the temperament types, the children are given scenarios to problem-solve, and the teachers are given strategies to effectively deal with children with each temperament type. As discussed previously, teachers are taught how to appropriately *scaffold and stretch* children so that they are working *with* children's temperaments, not against them, to help them reach goals or behave in an appropriate way.

McClowry and her colleagues (McClowry, Snow, & Tamis-LeMonda, 2005; O'Connor, Cappella, McCormick, & McClowry, 2014) have found consistent evidence to support the effectiveness of INSIGHTS for improving young children's behavior and academic skills. In addition, INSIGHTS seems to be particularly effective for shy children. Specifically, shy children in classrooms where the INSIGHTS program was implemented outperformed their peers in classrooms without INSIGHTS in both math and critical thinking skills. Shy children in INSIGHTS classrooms were also more engaged in classroom activities, which resulted in their better academic performance. Although INSIGHTS has yet to be tested outside of New York City, the principles and promise of this program suggest that teaching teachers and children about temperament and providing temperament-based strategies to help teachers individualize their interactions with children may be very effective for optimizing shy children's outcomes in school. More information about INSIGHTS can be found at insightsintervention.com/ and steinhardt.nyu.edu/insights/.

CONCLUSIONS

The general practices that we have outlined here for helping children who are experiencing anxiety due to shyness are intended to provide an overview of what has been shown to be successful beyond the classroom context. Several themes are clear: Helping shy children is a challenge involving patience and understanding, change does not happen overnight, and interventions geared toward helping individuals acknowledge and attend to feelings and thoughts seem very effective. We also saw that there are several evidence-based programs for implementation in classrooms. In the next chapter, we will move to specific strategies for teachers to use with shy children in their classrooms, many of which are based on best practices for working with all children.

CHAPTER 8

Best Practices for Assisting Shy Children

Part II: Specific Strategies

HELPING SHY CHILDREN—A TEACHER'S WORDS

I think of the girl especially that I taught last year, just how important it was to make sure that every dealing with her was on a level key and that every dealing with her built up her confidence. Because . . . not that we yell a lot, but if someone had yelled or snapped at her it would have just devastated her . . . you sort of hold her in the palm of your hand and watch her grow.

(Lao, Akseer, Bosacki, & Coplan, 2013, p. 276)

In this chapter, we describe a range of specific strategies that educators can employ to assist shy children in their classrooms. This chapter represents the culmination of everything we have addressed in this book until now. The techniques we discuss here are derived from the theory and research previously reviewed in this book and explicitly formulated for use with shy children during challenging situations at school. We also draw on several previous studies where researchers have asked teachers for their *best practices* in promoting positive outcomes among their shy students.

As you may recall, shy children's common behaviors at school include the refusal to speak or using quiet speech, a lack of eye contact, blushing, lower levels of engagement with peers, and failure to participate in classroom activities. As we have seen, common stressful circumstances at school that are most likely to evoke such behaviors among shy students include the following features: (1) novelty; (2) perceived evaluation; and (3) peers. For example, one of the most difficult experiences in school for shy children is the transition to school (as a kindergartner or as a new student). Although this is challenging for all students, shy children experience heightened stress during this transition because of how they strongly react to novelty and social situations, both of which abound at the start of school. In this chapter, we describe and discuss a series of specific strategies for assisting shy children in the classroom as they grapple with novelty, perceived evaluation, and peers.

COPING WITH NOVELTY

The start of the school year can be a time of excessive stress for shy children because there is so much that is new and unpredictable. There is uncertainty associated with almost everything, including a new teacher, classroom, classmates, routines, and expectations. So much novelty can be overwhelming for shy children, even when they are older and the newness of formal school has worn off. There are several strategies that teachers can employ to help ease the transition to school for shy children. Of course, many of these approaches will be helpful for all children, but some are particularly suited and effective for easing this transition for shy students. The different sets of strategies we describe are intended to help familiarize children with the new school and classroom environment, enhance communication between teachers, students, and parents, and implement classroom structures and processes that ease shy children's worry.

Familiarization with the School and Classroom

Much of the novelty of new school and classroom settings is about the physical features and layouts of these environments. Children often worry about the logistics of their surroundings, such as knowing where to go for class, the bathroom, the office, where they'll be met for pick-up or getting the bus after school, where to eat lunch, where they will put their belongings, where they will sit in class, who they will sit next to, and how they will buy lunch. Many of these concerns can be at least somewhat alleviated by visiting the school and classroom prior to the start of the school year. Ideally, children will be able to come with parents or another familiar caregiver to walk around the school, identify and locate various important places in the school, and see the classroom.

If possible, these visits should first take place in the prior school year, so that the child experiences the school setting when it is full of children (as it will be when the child starts school). Then, another visit should be arranged in the weeks immediately prior to the new school year, so the child has the opportunity to review the layout of the school, see his or her assigned classroom, and familiarize him- or herself with the location of the classroom in relation to other important locations, such as the bathroom. During one of these visits, children should also be able to view the classrooms where they will have other classes such as physical education and art. Ideally, these visits will also include opportunities to meet various teachers, as well as the principal, assistant principal, office staff, librarian, and other school personnel.

Typically, these orientation-type activities are organized before children start kindergarten, but they vary widely in the extent to which children are allowed to explore and interact with the school, as well as whether and to what extent parents are involved. They also are less often offered to children once they are beyond kindergarten age. Shy children are likely to need more than the typical level of exposure provided to students; teachers and principals should reach out to families to let them know that there are additional opportunities for children to visit the school and classrooms as needed, and encourage them to take advantage of these opportunities.

Enhancing Communication Among Teachers, Students, and Parents

In addition to opportunities for the child to visit the school and classroom, there should be opportunities for teachers to interact with children one-on-one *before* the school year begins. This can occur during a child's visit to the school for orientation-type activities, or it can occur in the child's home or at another venue. It is important that this one-on-one interaction time occurs without other children in the room or nearby, as they can cause unnecessary stress or distraction for the shy child (and the teacher). Whenever possible, talking directly with the child is better than just meeting the parent or caregiver; this will give the child a relatively lower stress opportunity to interact directly with the teacher as will be necessary during the regular school day. This is also an excellent time for teachers to reach out to parents to gather information about their children. Such information can be invaluable for the teacher in preparing to help children deal with fears or problems at the start of school and to facilitate social experiences with peers.

Another strategy is for teachers to call or email the families of all of the children assigned to them. This is helpful so that families will know how to reach their children's teachers, and provides an opportunity to send a clear message that teachers would like to hear from parents about their children. This may prompt parents of shy children (who as we have seen are often worried about their children's adjustment to new situations) to begin a constructive dialogue with teachers. However, some parents may not even be aware that their child's shyness could make the transition to school particularly difficult. Thus, asking specific questions to help parents think about these issues may facilitate the process of getting more helpful information. Whether initiated by parents or teachers, it is important to have two-way parent-teacher communication as early as possible so that parents and teachers can work together to help shy children be successful in school. This process works most efficiently when parents and teachers are on the same page.

Finally, as we will discuss in more detail in the next section, it is also helpful during these conversations to share with parents and children the daily routines and what to expect throughout the school day. For example, it may be a good idea to write down a daily routine or schedule for parents and children to use as a reference, especially during the first several weeks of the school year.

CASE STUDY: THE SAME OLD SAME OLD

Rosa was a shy child, but very happy in her 1st-grade class. Her teacher had a very warm and welcoming style, and Rosa was clear on where she had to be, what she should be doing, and when.

One day, Rosa's teacher was sick and called in for a substitute. For some reason, the substitute did not arrive by the beginning of the school day. The students in Rosa's class didn't miss a beat. As they arrived to school, they took their bags and coats to their cubbies, grabbed their journals, went to their desks, and began writing in response to the daily prompt which had been written on the chalkboard.

When the substitute teacher arrived about 15 minutes after school started, she thought she was in the wrong room. The children were quietly and busily working at their desks, and had hardly noticed that their teacher was absent; they had a well-established routine of what to do at the beginning of the day, and their teacher's expectations were quite clear.

Establishing Clear Classroom Routines and Expectations

A significant component of novelty-related stress for shy students is uncertainty about rules and routines, especially at the start of a new school year. Most children, but particularly those who are shy, are more successful in classrooms where behavioral expectations are clear and consistently enforced. Shy children are already more prone to being anxious about what they might view as inconsistent or arbitrary disciplinary action, and are likely to freeze up in response to that kind of uncertainty. To help alleviate such concerns, teachers should make classroom rules very clear from the beginning of the school year. This is not only good classroom management practice overall, but also particularly beneficial for shy children.

In addition, established classroom routines help to reduce stress among shy children. When children know what to expect on a typical day in the classroom, they have less fear about coming to school and moving through the day. Indeed, well-established routines benefit all students, as they allow for smooth transitions between activities and more efficient use of time.

Establishing and teaching routines and expectations will require a bigger time investment at the beginning of the year, but the payoff is that very little energy will be devoted to reminders about routines and expectations later in the year. As an added benefit, when an expected or unexpected event occurs that results in a change in the daily routines of the classroom (such as a substitute teacher, field trip, or schoolwide assembly), children will more easily adapt, confident that behavior expectations will not change, and that the disruption is temporary rather than normal (as illustrated in the case study at the outset of this section). Some specific suggestions for establishing clear classroom routines and expectations are provided in Box 8.1.

Of course, there will inevitably be changes in the classroom and school routines. Some of these will be anticipated and planned for ahead of time (such as field trips and school assemblies), whereas others are unexpected and thus unplanned (such as teacher illness or an emergency). Whenever possible, give children advance notice of changes in their regular routine. This should come via announcements made to the whole class and posted on the class calendar to help children be aware of upcoming events and able to count down to them. This advance notice should include information about what will change and what will be the same as usual, as well as instructions for behavior expectations that may be different because of different circumstances. As an example, for a field trip to see a live theater production, behavioral expectations would include reminders about the importance of being quiet and staying seated during the performance. Whereas advance notice should help all children adjust more smoothly to changes in the daily routine, this will be particularly helpful to shy children, who may worry about such change. It may be necessary to follow-up with shy children one-on-one about upcoming events or changes in the regular routine, because in a larger group format, shy children are unlikely to feel comfortable asking questions. Alternatively, a shy child could be partnered with another child to discuss the upcoming event (making use of peers to assist shy children in the classroom will be discussed in more detail in the next section).

Box 8.1. Clarifying Routines and Expectations

- Post and explain the regular daily schedule.
- Post a daily agenda and longer-term calendar that are available for student reference.
- Describe and remind students of classroom routines (for example: When you arrive in the morning, put your things away and start writing in your journal).
- Describe and remind students of behavioral expectations (for example: When the teacher or a classmate is talking, you should be listening).

The school context is in a state of constant flux. Although many children may be energized by this dynamic environment, for shy children, the accompanying uncertainty results in unease and stress. By striving (where possible) to incorporate a more predictable and organized structure to overlie this rapid change, teachers can help shy children better cope with the demands placed on them in these situations.

EASING EVALUATIVE CONCERNS

As we discussed in Chapter 6, shy children find classrooms nerve-racking, in part, because of the heavy emphasis on evaluation, both real and perceived. Of course, there is quite a bit of *real* evaluation by teachers that occurs in classrooms, and this causes some performance problems for shy children. However, shy children often have difficulty interacting with adults in positions of authority (such as teachers and other school personnel) because they *perceive* they are being evaluated, even when they are not. As we discuss next, reducing evaluative concerns can be accomplished by fostering rapport between teachers and shy children, and productively involving shy children in classroom discourse.

Get to Know Shy Children

A first critical step in alleviating evaluative concerns of shy children is to develop positive relationships with them, and that is best accomplished by getting to know them! As we discussed in depth in Chapter 6, getting to know the shy children in a classroom is often much easier said than done. However, there are several strategies that can be effective for facilitating this at the beginning of the school year. First, some schools require kindergarten teachers to make home visits to each child in their classrooms. This provides an excellent opportunity for teachers to identify shy children if they know what questions to ask of parents (and children) and what behaviors to look for when they meet the children. In their own homes, shy children may be less apt to feel wary and self-conscious (they have the home-field advantage!). Even so, the presence of an unfamiliar adult and authority figure is still likely to elicit shy behaviors. For example a child hiding behind a parent, showing an unwillingness to speak or speaking quietly, and reluctance to make eye contact will all be clear indicators that the child is also likely to display such behaviors in the classroom.

However, home visits are not typical, particularly as children move into grades beyond kindergarten. As an alternative, and as suggested earlier in this chapter, phone calls with parents can be helpful for getting more information about children. Another effective and relatively easy approach for getting information on students' shyness (and other behaviors and characteristics) is to give parents a brief survey about their child's interests, behaviors, and personality. This can be mailed or emailed to parents prior to the start of school, and then returned with other paperwork at the beginning of school when parents typically have other forms that they have to complete. We have also seen teachers distribute this type of survey at the back-to-school open house so that the information can be collected immediately. As children get older, it becomes more appropriate to give *them* the survey to complete. Children tend to enjoy answering surveys about themselves. Moreover, the written format and the fact that there are no right or wrong answers will help to reduce stress and thus yield more helpful responses from children. As children get older, information from them about their interests and personalities is more helpful than from parents, and this type of survey is often useful as a first-day-of-school activity as children are getting settled in the classroom.

Engage in Positive Interactions with Children

Beyond these initial efforts to get to know shy children better, another effective way of alleviating shy children's social-evaluative concerns is to interact with them in a way that shows acceptance independent of their performance or behavior in class. As Kathryn Wentzel (2002) noted in her work on students' success in classrooms, good teachers are very much like good parents: When teachers are warm and supportive, children thrive.

So how can teachers show this unconditional acceptance? This can come across in many different ways, such as smiling at children, using a positive speaking tone, meeting children at eye level, providing encouragement, and using polite and respectful language in conversation with children and adults in the classroom. Some additional specific strategies are listed in Box 8.2. A significant benefit of these strategies is that they facilitate the development of a positive teacher-student relationship. As we have seen, positive relationships between teachers and students promote children's long-term success both socially and academically, and are particularly helpful for the school adjustment of shy children.

Vary Ways for Children to Participate in the Classroom

As we discussed in Chapter 5, much of the instruction in typical elementary (and secondary) classrooms is conducted in large-group formats, where students are expected to raise their hands or be called on by the teacher to speak in front of the class. Since this entails being the momentary center of attention, and can evoke feelings of being *on-the-spot*, shy children tend to avoid involvement in such class discussions like the plague. However, there are other ways to encourage shy children's participation in classroom activities and discussions that are less threatening and, ultimately, may elicit more thoughtful responses from *all* students.

Box 8.2. Promoting Positive Interactions with Your Shy Students

- Greet students at the door of the classroom by name each day.

  This ensures that each student has at least one interaction with the teacher each day, and starts the day off on a positive note.

- Ask students about their extracurricular activities and interests.

  Learning about the activities students are involved in outside of school can be very eye-opening for understanding what motivates them in the classroom, and may be helpful for encouraging shy children to step out of their comfort zone.

- Privately recognize shy children's accomplishments inside and outside of the classroom.

  Students who believe that their teachers care about their accomplishments are likely to try harder in the future—this can facilitate a shy child's progress toward adjusting to the classroom and feeling more comfortable with the teacher.

One approach is to first have students take a moment to write down ideas or responses before being asked to share them with the class. As an additional buffer, students can share their written responses with a partner, and then the pair of students can make a decision about what to share with the class (which then becomes something they can share together). There are other versions of this that can work with younger children. For example, children could draw a picture of their ideas and then talk about their pictures with a partner, or produce a joint picture that depicts the ideas they both have. These types of approaches, where students have time to think, then get feedback on their thoughts, and then share with other children, allow shy children to be more meaningfully engaged in classroom discussion (and in a structured format with peers) in a less threatening way. This approach also draws upon the practice of graduated exposure (which we described in Chapter 7), by encouraging shy children to work up to speaking in front of a group by first sharing with one or a few other students, then sharing the information that the group agreed upon with the class. A particularly effective method of this that we have used is called *think-pair-share*, which is described in detail in Box 8.3.

Another way to encourage shy children's participation, and to engage more children in general, is to have students signal responses to questions nonverbally. This can serve to help even the playing field for shy children, who are often reticent at first to speak aloud in front of others. A variety of such responses can be incorporated, involving gestures (e.g., thumbs up/

Box 8.3. Think-Pair-Share

- Place children into groups of four, each comprised of two sets of pairs.
- Direct all students to respond independently in writing to a prompt (e.g., What is the main idea of the story we just read?) (suggested time: 1–3 minutes).
- Have students share their written responses in their pairs. They should discuss their responses, not just read them to each other, and merge their responses so that they have one new pair response (suggested time: 3–5 minutes).
- Have students share their pair responses with the other pair in their group. Again, they should discuss their responses, not just read them to each other, and merge their responses so they have one new group response (suggested time: 3–5 minutes).
- Have 1 person from each group share their response with the class.

---

down/sideways to indicate yes/no/maybe) or signs that students hold up (e.g., yes/no, true/false, or A/B/C/D). Teachers' questions to students can be to gather information about general understanding of a concept (for example, "Who knows the difference between an adjective and an adverb?") or to solicit opinions from the class ("Should we read *Charlotte's Web*?"). There are also increasing opportunities to use electronic devices for instant and anonymous classroom response feedback—these systems allow students to respond to teacher questions using multiple-choice or true/false formats. Responses are immediately recorded and displayed so the teacher and students see the rates of response and understanding, agreement, or opinion among students. The anonymous nature of these electronic response systems makes them even more appealing for shy children than signs or hand gestures, but they require purchasing hardware and software.

Signs, signals, and electronic response systems are less useful for class discussions. Thus, for more complex topics requiring student input beyond yes/no or objective responses, children can provide anonymous questions, comments, or responses in a question box prior to the class discussion. The teacher (or students) can then read them aloud and incorporate them into a class discussion.

Teacher Talk

In large-group settings, such as show-and-tell and circle time, teachers tend to ask shy children a lot of direct questions. Indeed, research suggests that the less children speak, the more likely teachers are to ask them questions! Frequent questioning may be intimidating to shy children because it reinforces the notion of teacher as an authority figure. So teachers may actually unintentionally suppress their shy students' willingness to share. Teachers can stimulate lengthier verbal responses from shy children by asking fewer questions and, instead, adding *phatics* (statements of agreement, such as "uh-huh" and "oh,") or shared experience (such as "me too") when shy children are speaking. As we described previously, researcher Mary Ann Evans (Evans & Bienert, 1992) found that shy kindergartners were much more likely to speak and elaborate on their talking points during show-and-tell when teachers used more phatics and fewer direct questions, and were careful to allow a bit of extra time for these children to respond.

Teachers can also encourage children to talk more by initiating games in which they are required to take speaking turns. For example, a game like "Go Fish" requires children to take turns asking for cards and responding to queries for cards. In this way, shy children have the opportunity to speak and will not just get overtaken by the more talkative children. Of course, there will be times when teachers *do* need to ask shy children direct questions. One strategy is to ask shy children questions that the teacher is sure they can respond to; this helps slowly build their confidence. Teachers can then praise shy children for speaking (and for other positive social behaviors). However, teachers should remain mindful to not draw too much attention to shy children when offering them praise (recall that being the center of attention, even for positive reasons, tends to make shy children feel self-conscious), and consider praising shy children less overtly in the moment, and instead use a smile, wink, gesture, or other subtle means, or give praise after class.

Optimizing Testing Situations

Shy children have a tendency to *perceive* that they are being evaluated in situations where evaluation is not actually happening. Of course, in educational settings, there are regular occasions when shy children are in fact being evaluated. In Chapter 5, we discussed some of the ways that testing situations can elicit feelings of anxiety and performance difficulties for shy children. As we described, research by Ray Crozier (Crozier & Perkins, 2002; Crozier & Hostettler, 2003) suggests that individually administered assessments (i.e., one-on-one with the tester) appear to be particularly stressful for shy children. Thus, teachers may not necessarily be doing shy children a favor when they suggest presenting their oral report directly to the teacher during recess instead of in front of the entire class.

We do not think it is particularly realistic to suggest to teachers that they should modify and adapt their testing protocols to specifically suit the characteristics of each individual student in their class. However, teachers should certainly be aware of how shy children's characteristics might impact their performance in testing situations and, with this in mind, attempt to accommodate where feasible. For example, teachers are encouraged to use group-administered written tests when possible because they appear to be less stressful for shy children than other formats, such as individually administered tests.

Small accommodations can also pay large dividends. For example, the more *anonymous* testing situations are, the less likely they will be stressful and problematic for shy children. One way to increase this sense of anonymity is to give students temporary privacy barriers to use during testing so that they feel secure that no one is watching or evaluating them while they are writing their answers. Another relatively small accommodation, and good teaching practice, is to give children study guides for test preparation. Anxiety about test content will be reduced when shy children have something tangible to reference as they prepare for the test. In the case of oral presentations, teachers should engage shy students in a private conversation ahead of time, where they acknowledge to the children that they understand that this is stressful for them (and point out that public speaking is stressful for lots of people). The teacher can also offer support and encouragement, as well as specific strategies for how the students might prepare (e.g., practice in front of a mirror).

PROMOTING POSITIVE SOCIAL INTERACTIONS WITH PEERS

As we have seen, the mere presence of peers is stressful for shy children. Moreover, the classroom is particularly fraught with stress for shy children because it is a context that not only includes many peers, but also demands interaction with peers. There are several strategies that teachers can use to decrease the stress of dealing with peers in the classroom. Like many of the other recommendations in this chapter, suggestions for assisting shy children are also sound classroom management techniques.

Decrease Uncertainty

One reason peers in the classroom evoke stress among shy children is because of the *uncertainty* involved. Shy students are prone to worry about interacting with peers in the classroom ("Who will be my partner?" "Who will I sit with?" "Will anyone want to play with me?"). As we have seen, such concerns, as well as a general discomfort about initiating social interactions, can be both anxiety-provoking and distracting. Thus, decreasing uncertainty in interactions with peers is important and can dramatically reduce stress for shy children (and chaos in the classroom in general!).

An example of one way to do this is for teachers to consider assigning students to partners or groups, as opposed to telling students to "pick a partner" or "turn to your neighbor." This is not only less stressful for shy children, but it is also more efficient for getting classroom activities moving. This practice also eliminates problems with someone (often a shy child) being left without a partner, which calls additional attention to that child, further intensifying stress and embarrassment. An added benefit of teachers selecting partners is that it will prevent more boisterous and exuberant children from being partnered with other such children (which can make for more classroom disruptions). The practice of teacher-assigned partners and groups also places the perception of problems between peers/partners on the teacher, rather than on the children. This serves to direct potentially negative attention (and stress) away from the shy child (i.e., it is the teacher's fault that we are stuck together, so let's just make the best of it).

Find Strategic Partners and Mentors

Another approach is to strategically partner shy children with more sociable or outgoing children, which can be particularly effective for the first few days of school. These partners sit together and manage the first several days' tasks together, navigating the unfamiliar classroom (and school) as a team. This has the benefit of facilitating a peer relationship for the shy child, through the bonding experience of facing the challenging first days of school. This will also potentially broaden the shy child's peer network through association with a more outgoing peer who already possesses abilities to build peer networks. It also fosters more outgoing children's understanding of their shy peers and promotes peer acceptance, and possibly friendship, between children who may have been less likely to forge relationships.

If possible, shy children should be paired with peers who are somewhat sensitive and not too extroverted (which can overwhelm a shy child's withdrawn nature). It may also be helpful for teachers to be mindful of some of our research (Arbeau, Coplan, & Matheson, 2012) showing that older shy kids may have a tendency to be overly dependent on some of their friends—using them as *social surrogates* (e.g., having a friend talk *for* them in social situations). It is therefore important to facilitate strategic partnerships that are relatively balanced so that the shy child does not become dependent on the other child for successful social interactions.

Similarly, teachers may want to employ peer *mentors*. Often used in secondary school settings, we see peer mentors used less often in elementary school settings. However, there is a very clear place for them. Peer mentors can be either older or same-age children who have excellent leadership skills, enjoy interacting with other children, and are gifted at putting other children at ease or making them feel welcome. Teachers can also turn to these mentors when a shy child needs support in the classroom during a stressful situation.

There does not need to be an official peer mentoring program in the school to use peers as mentors in the classroom. Remember the discussion earlier of using peers to help a shy child prepare for change in the classroom or an upcoming event? That would be a possible use for a peer mentor. A significant advantage to using this approach is that later in the school year, or in a future year, a shy child could be in this role for another child who is new to the classroom or to the school!

Monitoring Peer Interactions in the Classroom

Finally, it is very easy for teachers to become busy and for shy children's peer interactions (or lack thereof) to go unnoticed. Thus, it is particularly important for teachers to continue to monitor the interactions among children in their classrooms, paying particular attention to shy children's involvement in peer conversation and activities. Shy children are often quite adept at flying under the radar at school. Although remaining invisible to teachers and other children may help to reduce immediate feelings of stress in the short term, this is ultimately damaging to shy children's longer-term social and academic success.

As we saw in Chapter 3, shy children's reluctance to engage with peers and others in social interactions can quickly snowball into a pattern of behavior where lack of interaction begets incompetence with interaction, resulting in even greater reluctance to engage in interactions. Thus, it is critical that teachers are vigilant to this type of behavior in shy children so that they can intervene when necessary (the earlier in the school year, the better).

CONCLUSIONS

The types of challenges that the typical classroom presents to shy children—novelty, social evaluation, interacting with peers—can be met with specific strategies to help children successfully face these challenges. Some strategies, such as setting up strategic partners between shy and less shy peers and giving subtle or private praise to shy children for small successes, are intended specifically for assisting shy children. However, many of these strategies, such as engaging in positive interactions with students and having clear routines, are indicative of good teaching practice in general. All of these strategies require teachers to be actively engaged in the most important part of a teacher's job—getting to know the children in her classroom (see Box 8.4).

Box 8.4. Strategy Quick-Reference List

Coping with Novelty

- Familiarize child with teacher and classroom
- Enhance communication among teachers, children, and parents
- Establish clear routines and expectations

Easing Evaluative Concerns

- Get to know shy (and all) children
- Display warmth and acceptance
- Understand shy children's unique characteristics
- Vary ways children participate in classroom activities
- Optimize testing situations

Promoting Positive Interactions with Peers

- Decrease uncertainty in peer situations
- Use strategic partners
- Use peer mentors
- Monitor the classroom interactions

CHAPTER 9

Looking Forward

Shy Children in a Brave New World

CASE STUDY: THE FUTURE IS NOW

Jason is standing by his locker, ruminating, worrying, and stewing about how he is going to work up the courage to ask someone to the school dance. Lost in his thoughts, he is a bit startled when his phone beeps. He looks down at the screen to see a text message from Erica, asking him if he would like to go to the dance with her.

Despite being flustered, blushing, and tongue-tied, Jason carefully types in a response of "yes," and spends the rest of the day smiling to himself.

As we reach the final chapter of this book, we first take a moment to review briefly some of the key take-away messages from the previous chapters. To date, we have certainly learned a lot about the development of shyness in childhood and its implications for school adjustment. However, there are still many unanswered questions and much future work to be done. Moreover, the rapidly changing nature of contemporary society has tremendous implications for shy children. With this in mind, we then discuss shyness from the perspective of changing gender-role attitudes, similarities and differences in shyness across cultures, and the potential impact of emerging technologies on shy children's social interactions.

LOOKING BACK:
KEY TAKE-AWAY MESSAGES FROM THIS BOOK

We have presented you with a lot of information in this book. Before looking ahead to some future directions in our understanding of shyness in childhood, let's recap some of the main points raised in each of the previous chapters.

Chapter 1. What Is Shyness?

- Shyness is a temperamental trait that appears early in life and is relatively stable across development.
- Shy children tend to be wary when meeting new people and self-conscious when they are the center of attention.
- Shy children often want to interact with others, but this social motivation conflicts with their feelings of fear and anxiety in social situations.

Chapter 2. The Nature of Shyness: Genetics and Biological Foundations

- Although there is no single gene for shyness, at least a part of shyness appears to be heritable.
- Many shy children have a nervous system that seems to be wired like a tightly-coiled spring that is easily set off by social stressors.
- Biology is not destiny: Shy children's experiences in the family and at school are also extremely influential contributors to their social, emotional, and academic well-being.

Chapter 3. Nurtured to Be Shy: Attachment and Parenting

- Shy children may develop a general view of the world as a scary and unpredictable place.
- Parents may inadvertently exacerbate shy children's fears by modeling anxious behaviors, highlighting threats in the environment, and engaging in overprotective parenting.
- Teachers should keep in mind that shy parents are likely to be particularly worried about their shy children, whereas non-shy parents often have difficulty understanding their child's shy behaviors, thoughts, and emotions.

Chapter 4. Costs and Benefits of Shyness for Children's Development

- Because they spend comparatively more time alone, shy children may miss out on many of the important and unique benefits of peer interaction for children's development.
- Extremely shy children are at increased risk for the later development of more serious mental health difficulties, including anxiety disorders and depression.
- Notwithstanding, it is important to note that there are many positive aspects to shyness, and many shy children grow up to do just fine.

Chapter 5. Shy Children in the Classroom

- The dynamic and social nature of the typical elementary classroom environment can make it a stressful and scary place for shy children.
- Shy children tend to not perform as well academically as their less-shy peers, particularly in areas requiring language or verbal performance, and may also seem unengaged in classroom activities.
- Shy children are particularly intimidated by classroom situations where there is real or perceived evaluation, such as performance or testing situations.

Chapter 6. Shy Children and Teachers

- Teachers shape the emotional climate of the classroom, and a positive emotional climate can be helpful for shy children.
- Teachers have difficulty getting to know shy children, which can contribute to more negative perceptions of shy children's abilities or interest.
- Shy children are less likely than their non-shy peers to have positive relationships with their teachers, yet positive teacher-child relationships can be particularly helpful and supportive for shy children in the school setting.

Chapter 7. Best Practices for Assisting Shy Children—Part I: General Approaches

- Helping shy children requires patience and understanding: change does not happen overnight.
- Techniques adapted from clinical approaches used to help individuals with anxiety (e.g., graduated exposure, cognitive behavior therapy, mindfulness) can be effectively applied to help shy children in the classroom.
- There are several classroom-based programs for helping shy and socially anxious children that have or are gaining evidence of effectiveness.

Chapter 8. Best Practices for Assisting Shy Children—Part II: Specific Strategies

- To help shy children deal with novelty in the classroom, provide advance opportunities to see the school and meet the teacher, facilitate communication between teacher, students, and parents, and establish clear routines and expectations.
- To ease evaluation concerns shy children often have in the classroom, make a concerted effort to get to know all students, display warmth and

acceptance, understand shy children's unique characteristics and needs, vary the ways in which children can participate in classroom activities, and optimize testing situations.

- To promote shy children's positive peer interactions, decrease uncertainty in peer situations, use strategic partners and peer mentors, and monitor classroom interactions.

LOOKING FORWARD: CH-CH-CH-CH-CHANGES

The last 25 years have been witness to a huge growth in research interest about the development and implication of shyness in childhood. This increased attention is fostering raised awareness about shyness among parents, teachers, and others. However, not only do gaps remain in our knowledge, but ongoing societal changes are opening up new avenues for consideration. In this section, we provide a brief discussion of some of these emerging new directions, which we think will be important for teachers to keep in mind in their future interactions with shy children in the classroom.

Bashful Boys Versus Coy Girls

Are there *gender* differences in shyness? By now, you may not be surprised to learn that, like many other features of shyness, the answer to this seemingly simple question is actually quite complex. The first aspect to consider is whether the overall prevalence, frequency, or amount of shyness is different between boys and girls. That is, are girls generally more shy than boys—or vice versa?

The answer to this is, mostly, *no*. When we measure shyness using parent reports, teacher reports, peer ratings, or observations, there is typically no gender difference evident. However, the exception here is self-reports of shyness among older children. In late childhood and adolescence, girls actually report higher overall levels of shyness than boys. There are several possible reasons for this. For example, it may be because girls at this age are becoming more prone to anxiety, depression, and other internalizing problems (it is well-established that females are more likely to suffer from internalizing disorders than males, and this begins in adolescence). Alternatively, it may also be that boys are more likely to understate their shyness when reporting to others (for a recent review see Doey, Coplan, & Kingsbury, 2014).

This second explanation may be partially accounted for by societal pressures and expectations regarding gender stereotypes. Indeed, it has been suggested that shyness is less socially acceptable for boys than for girls because shy behaviors and emotions violate gender norms related to male social assertiveness and dominance. This leads to another type of question about gender and shyness: Does shyness have different *implications* for boys versus girls? The answer to this question appears to be *yes,* at least to some degree. For example, there is some evidence to suggest that shy behaviors in girls are more likely to be rewarded and accepted by parents, whereas shyness in boys is more likely to be discouraged and result in more negative interactions. Similarly, shy boys are more likely to be excluded and rejected by peers than shy girls (see Doey et al., 2014). Interestingly, the same has *not* generally been found for teachers. That is, some of our previous studies of teachers' attitudes about, responses to, and relationships with shy children have not typically shown gender differences (Coplan, Bullock, Archbell, & Bosacki, 2015; Coplan, Hughes, Bosacki, & Rose-Krasnor, 2011). Perhaps teacher training and experiences come to override gender stereotypes regarding shyness.

Moreover, as illustrated in the case study at the outset of this chapter, in contemporary society, traditional gender-norms, stereotypes, and beliefs appear to be increasingly eroding. For example, in a classic study of U.S. babies born in the late 1920s, researcher Avshalom Caspi and his colleagues found that men who were shy as boys married, started families, and entered stable careers later than their non-shy counterparts (Caspi, Bem, & Elder, 1988). In contrast, no such differences were found for women. However, in a more recent longitudinal study of German youth, researcher Jens Asendorpf and his colleagues reported a similar pattern of life delays for *both* men and women who were shy as children (Asendorpf, Denissen, & van Aken, 2008).

For teachers, it will be important to consider issues of gender in their classrooms. Although teachers appear to be less likely to act upon potential gender stereotypes regarding childhood shyness, shy boys and girls may still be treated differently by peers, parents, and society. Thus, sensitivity to subtle (or not so subtle) variations in the ways that shyness plays out in boys' and girls' behaviors may be key, particularly as children age. For example, as adolescents become more attuned to societal expectations for appropriate gender-stereotyped behavior, shy girls may be even more at-risk than shy boys for withdrawing from social discourse in the classroom, especially in typically male-dominated subjects such as science.

It's a Shy, Shy World

Almost all of the research on shyness that we have talked about in this book so far has been conducted in North America or Western Europe. In recent years, there has been a tremendous increase in research about children's shyness in non-Western cultures. It is now increasingly understood that the meaning and implications of shyness (and many other social behaviors) can vary significantly across *cultures.*

For example, in traditional Chinese society, wariness and behavioral restraint tend to be more positively evaluated and even highly encouraged. Indeed, shy and quiet behaviors are considered respectful, and are thought to reflect humbleness, social maturity, and understanding. In support of this notion (and in contrast to results found in Western societies), researcher Xinyin Chen and others have previously reported that, as compared to their non-shy counterparts, shy children in China tended to do better academically, were more popular among classmates, and were viewed as leaders and model students by their teachers (Chen, Rubin, & Li, 1995).

However, over the last 20 years, China has been experiencing large-scale economic reforms and dramatic societal changes. As a result, Chen and others (Chen, Cen, Li, & He, 2005) have suggested that behavioral characteristics such as initiative and self-expression might be becoming more adaptive in contemporary China to adjust to this more competitive environment. Relatedly, the adaptive value of shy behavior in China may also be declining. In support of these ideas, and in sharp contrast to previous findings, results from the most recent research indicates that shyness in large urban areas in China is now associated with socio-emotional difficulties, including peer rejection, a lack of leadership at school, and symptoms of depression (Ding et al., 2014; Liu et al., 2014). It is fascinating to see how quickly these economic and societal changes have filtered down to the level of valued childhood behaviors. Nonetheless, in rural areas, where such changes have largely not been felt as yet, shyness remains positively valued and associated with positive outcomes at school (Chen, Wang, & Cao, 2011). It remains to be seen how such changes might be manifested in these areas in the future.

Ongoing trends toward multiethnic and multicultural classrooms means that it will also become increasingly important for teachers to consider cultural issues related to shyness. For example, although expectations for behavior in Western classrooms include willingness to speak up, volunteer, and answer questions in front of the class, teachers should keep in mind that variations in children's behavior may stem from different cultural values that may emphasize a more quiet or submissive style to show respect. We've focused in this volume on shyness as a characteristic that is part of a child's temperament or personality. However, although culturally manifested shy behaviors may look similar, the roots of these behaviors and the internal processes that underlie their display are very different.

Shy Versus Social Networks

Finally, perhaps the greatest ongoing changes in contemporary society involve the incredibly rapid advances in technology, particularly around computer-mediated communications and social networks. The effects of our transition into the information age are only just beginning to be studied and are far from understood. Indeed, change is so rapid that research into the effects of technology seems outdated nearly as soon as it is published!

There are competing theories about what this might mean for the social lives of shy children and adolescents. On the one hand, there is the *social compensation* hypothesis, which states that shy, introverted, and socially anxious individuals may turn to the Internet to communicate with and form relationships with peers. That is, computer-mediated forms of communication can provide shy individuals with a less anxiety-provoking context for social interactions. For example, as also illustrated in the case study at the outset of this chapter, communicating via text messages can relieve some of the stresses of social interaction for shy children. In this communicating context, shy individuals do not have to worry about any physical manifestations of their social anxiety (e.g., blushing, stumbling on their words), and can pause and consider their responses without feeling as if they are under social scrutiny. The anonymous nature of some Internet-based communications may also help shy individuals explore their identity in a safe environment, work through feelings of self-consciousness, and hone social skills. These experiences might then translate into more successful face-to-face social interactions.

In contrast, there is also the *rich-get-richer* hypothesis, which suggests that sociable, outgoing, and extroverted individuals will benefit most from the Internet as a social medium. The idea here is that individuals who already have good social skills and many friends will use computer-mediated communications to further strengthen their existing social networks in the real world. By comparison, shy and socially anxious people are thought to gain less from Internet interactions and will simply find this yet another context where they are less socially adept. Moreover, shy children might also worsen their real-world social relationships by retreating to the perceived reduced stress of on-line and virtual communications.

As such technologies increasingly make their way into the classroom, teachers should be mindful of their impact on shy students. There is increasing pressure on teachers to use technology in their classrooms. Indeed, in some school districts, students are even being supplied with tablets or laptops to facilitate their ready use of technology. Many teachers use social media–type platforms for students to connect with them, one another, and the broader academic community. The expectations for technology use are increasing almost as rapidly in schools as in society at large. Depending on the ways shy children interact with social media and technology, whether it is, indeed, *social compensation* or *rich get richer*, these technologies may even the playing field for shy children or exacerbate the differences between them and their more outgoing peers. Either way, use of advancing technologies in the classroom is another place teachers should be aware that shy children may respond differently than other students. Sensitivity and attunement will be important for teachers moving forward into this realm.

A FINAL MESSAGE

Children's school lives, especially in the elementary grades, lay the groundwork and establish the trajectory for their future. Yet it is helpful to remember that children are resilient. They have ways of letting us know what they need if we know how to pay attention to the messages they are sending. It is our hope that this text has provided a manual for reading shy students' messages—that the signals will now be clearer and the way forward will be easier.

References

Ainsworth, M. D. S., Blehar, M. C., Waters, E., & Wall, S. (1978). *Patterns of attachment: Assessed in the strange situation and at home*. Hillsdale, NJ: Erlbaum.

American Psychiatric Association. (2013). *Diagnostic and statistical manual of mental disorders* (5th ed.). Washington, DC: American Psychiatric Press.

Arbeau, K. A., Coplan, R. J., & Matheson, A. (2012). Someone to lean on: Assessment and implications of social surrogate use in childhood. *Social Development, 21,* 254–272.

Arbeau, K. A., Coplan, R. J., & Weeks M. (2010). Shyness, teacher-child relationships, and socio-emotional adjustment in grade 1. *International Journal of Behavioral Development, 34,* 259–269.

Arcus, D. (1989). Vulnerability and eye color in Disney cartoon characters. In J. S. Reznick (Ed.), *Perspectives on behavioral inhibition* (pp. 291–297). Chicago, IL: University of Chicago Press.

Asendorpf, J. (1990). Beyond social withdrawal: Shyness, unsociability and peer avoidance. *Human Development, 33,* 250–259.

Asendorpf, J. B., Denissen, J. J. A., & van Aken, M. A. G. (2008). Inhibited and aggressive preschool children at 23 years of age: Personality and social transitions into adulthood. *Developmental Psychology, 44,* 997–1011.

Baer, R. A. (2014). *Mindfulness-based treatment approaches: Clinician's guide to evidence base and applications*. Waltham, MA: Academic Press.

Bandura, A. (1977). *Social learning theory*. Englewood Cliffs, NJ: Prentice-Hall.

Barrett, P. M., & Turner, C. (2001). Prevention of anxiety symptoms in primary school children: Preliminary results from a universal schoolbased trial. *British Journal of Clinical Psychology, 40,* 399–410.

Battaglia, M., Ogliari, A., Zanoni, A., Citterio, A., Pozzoli, U., Giora, R., et al. (2005). Influence of the serotonin transporter promoter gene and shyness on children's cerebral responses to facial expressions. *Archives of General Psychiatry, 62,* 85–94.

Baumrind, D. (1975). Some thoughts about childrearing. In U. Bronfenbrenner & M. A. Mahoney (Eds.), *Influences on human development* (pp. 270–282). Hinsdale, IL: The Dryden Press.

Beaton, E. A., Schmidt, L. A., Schulkin, J., Antony, M. M., Swinson, R. P., & Hall, G. B. (2008). Different neural responses to stranger and personally familiar faces in shy and bold adults. *Behavioral Neuroscience, 122,* 704–709.

Bohlin, G., Hagekull, B., & Andersson, K. (2005). Behavioral inhibition as a precursor of peer social competence in early school age: The interplay with attachment and nonparental care. *Merrill-Palmer Quarterly, 51,* 1–19.

Booth-LaForce, C., & Oxford, M. L. (2008). Trajectories of social withdrawal from grades 1 to 6: Prediction from early parenting, attachment, and temperament. *Developmental Psychology, 44*(5), 1298–1313.

Bosacki, S. L., Coplan, R. J., Rose-Krasnor, L., & Hughes, K. (2011). Elementary school teachers' reflections on shy children in the classroom. *Alberta Journal of Educational Research, 57*, 273–287.

Bowlby, J. (1973). *Attachment and loss: Vol. 2. Separation: Anxiety and anger.* New York, NY: Basic Books.

Boyce, W. T., O'Neill-Wagner, P., Price, C. S., Haines, M., & Suomi, S. J. (1998). Crowding stress and violent injuries among behaviorally inhibited rhesus macaques. *Health Psychology, 17*, 285–289.

Buhs, E. S., Rudasill, K. M., Kalutskaya, I. N., & Griese, E. R. (2015). Shyness and engagement: Contributions of peer rejection and teacher sensitivity. *Early Childhood Research Quarterly, 30*, 12–19.

Burstein, M., & Ginsburg, G. S. (2010). The effect of parental modeling of anxious behaviors and cognitions in school-aged children: An experimental pilot study. *Behaviour Research and Therapy, 48*, 506–513.

Buss, A. H. (1986). Two kinds of shyness. In R. Schwarzer (Ed.), *Self-related cognitions in anxiety and motivation*. Hillsdale, NJ: Erlbaum.

Cain, S. (2012). *Quiet: The power of introverts in a world that can't stop talking.* New York, NY: Crown Publishers.

Campbell, H. (1896). Morbid shyness. *The British Medical Journal, 2*, 805–807.

Caspi, A., Bem, D. J., & Elder, G. H. (1988). Moving away from the world: Life-course patterns of shy children. *Developmental Psychology, 24*, 824–831.

Chen, X., Cen, G., Li, D., & He, Y. (2005). Social functioning and adjustment in Chinese children: The imprint of historical time. *Child Development, 76*, 182–195.

Chen, X., DeSouza, A., Chen, H., & Wang, L. (2006). Reticent behavior and experiences in peer interactions in Canadian and Chinese children. *Developmental Psychology, 42*, 656–665.

Chen, X., Rubin, K. H., & Li, B. (1995). Social and school adjustment of shy and aggressive children in China. *Development and Psychopathology, 7*, 337–349.

Chen, X., Wang, L., & Cao, R. (2011). Shyness-sensitivity and unsociability in rural Chinese children: Relations with social, school, and psychological adjustment. *Child Development, 82*, 1531–1543.

Christopher, J. S., Hansen, D. J., & MacMillan, V. M. (1991). Effectiveness of a peer-helper intervention to increase children's social interactions: Generalization, maintenance, and social validity. *Behavior Modification, 15*, 22–50.

Chronis-Tuscano, A., Degnan, K. A., Pine, D. S., Pérez-Edgar, K., Henderson, H. A., Diaz, Y., Raggi, V. L., & Fox, N. A. (2009). Stable early maternal report of behavioral inhibition predicts lifetime social anxiety disorder in adolescence. *Journal of the American Academy of Child & Adolescent Psychiatry, 48*, 928–935.

Chronis-Tuscano, A., Rubin, K. H., O'Brien, K. A., Coplan, R. J., Thomas, S. R., Dougherty, L. R., et al. (2015). Preliminary evaluation of a multimodal early intervention program for behaviorally inhibited preschoolers. *Journal of Consulting and Clinical Psychology, 83*, 534–540.

Chung, J. Y. Y., & Evans, M. A. (2000). Shyness and symptoms of illness in young children. *Canadian Journal of Behavioural Science, 32*, 49–57.

Clauss, J. A., & Blackford, J. U. (2012). Behavioral inhibition and the risk for developing social anxiety disorder: A meta-analytic study. *Journal of the American Academy of Child and Adolescent Psychiatry, 51*, 1066–1075.

Clifford, S., Lemery-Chalfant, K., & Goldsmith, H. H. (2015). The unique and shared genetic and environmental contributions to fear, anger, and sadness in childhood. *Child Development, 5*, 1538–1556.

Colonnesi, C., Napoleone, E., & Bögels, S. M. (2014). Positive and negative expressions of shyness in toddlers: Are they related to anxiety in the same way? *Journal of Personality and Social Psychology, 106*, 624–637.

Compton, S. N., March, J. S., Brent, D., Albano, A. M., Weersing, R., & Curry, J. (2004). Cognitive-behavioral psychotherapy for anxiety and depressive disorders in children and adolescents: An evidence-based medicine review. *Journal of the American Academy of Child & Adolescent Psychiatry, 43*, 930–959.

Coplan, R. J. & Arbeau, K. A. (2008). The stresses of a brave new world: Shyness and adjustment in kindergarten. *Journal of Research in Childhood Education, 22*, 377–389.

Coplan, R. J., Arbeau, K. A., & Armer, M. (2008). Don't fret, be supportive! Maternal characteristics linking child shyness to psychosocial and school adjustment in kindergarten. *Journal of Abnormal Child Psychology, 36*, 359–371.

Coplan, R. J., & Armer, M. (2005). "Talking yourself out of being shy": Shyness, expressive vocabulary, and adjustment in preschool. *Merrill-Palmer Quarterly, 51*, 20–41.

Coplan, R. J., Bullock, A., Archbell, K., & Bosacki, S. (2015). Preschool teachers' attitudes, beliefs, and emotional reactions to young children's peer group behaviors. *Early Childhood Research Quarterly, 30*, 117–127.

Coplan, R. J., Coleman, B., & Rubin, K. H. (1998). Shyness and Little Boy Blue: Iris pigmentation, gender, and social wariness in preschoolers. *Developmental Psychobiology, 32*, 37–44.

Coplan, R. J., & Evans, M. A. (2009). At a loss for words? Introduction to the special issue on shyness and language in childhood. *Infant and Child Development, 18*, 211–215.

Coplan, R. J., Findlay, L. C., & Nelson, L. J. (2004). Characteristics of preschoolers with lower perceived competence. *Journal of Abnormal Child Psychology, 32*, 399–408.

Coplan, R. J., Girardi, A., Findlay, L. C., & Frohlick, S. L. (2007). Understanding solitude: Young children's attitudes and responses towards hypothetical socially-withdrawn peers. *Social Development, 16*, 390–409.

Coplan, R. J., Hughes, K., Bosacki, S., & Rose-Krasnor, L. (2011). Is silence golden? Elementary school teachers' strategies and beliefs regarding hypothetical shy/quiet and exuberant/talkative children. *Journal of Educational Psychology, 103*, 939–951.

Coplan, R. J., Hughes, K., & Rowsell, H. C. (2010). Once upon a time there were a blushful hippo and a meek mouse: A content analysis of shy characters in young children's storybooks. In K. H. Rubin & R. J. Coplan (Eds.), *The development of shyness and social withdrawal* (pp. 262–276). New York, NY: Guilford.

Coplan, R. J., Ooi, L. L., & Nocita, G. (2015). When one is company and two is a crowd: Why some children prefer solitude. *Child Development Perspectives, 9*, 133–137.

Coplan, R. J., Ooi, L. L., & Rose-Krasnor, L. (2015). Naturalistic observations of schoolyard social participation: Marker variables for socio-emotional functioning in early adolescence. *Journal of Early Adolescence, 35,* 628–650.

Coplan, R. J., & Prakash, K. (2003). Spending time with teacher: Characteristics of preschoolers who frequently elicit versus initiate interactions with teachers. *Early Childhood Research Quarterly, 18,* 143–158.

Coplan, R. J., Reichel, M., & Rowan, K. (2009). Exploring the associations between maternal personality, child temperament, and parenting: A focus on emotions. *Personality and Individual Differences, 46,* 241–246.

Coplan, R. J. & Rubin, K. H. (2010). Social withdrawal and shyness in childhood: History, theories, definitions, and assessments. In K. H. Rubin & R. J. Coplan (Eds.), *The development of shyness and social withdrawal* (pp. 3–22). New York: Guilford.

Coplan, R. J., Schneider, B. H., Matheson, A., & Graham, A. A. (2010). "Play skills" for shy children: Development of a social skills-facilitated play early intervention program for extremely inhibited preschoolers. *Infant and Child Development, 19,* 223–237.

Coplan, R. J. & Weeks, M. (2009). Shy and soft-spoken? Shyness, pragmatic language, and socio-emotional adjustment in early childhood. *Infant and Child Development, 18,* 238–254.

Crozier, W. R. (1995). Shyness and self-esteem in middle childhood. *British Journal of Educational Psychology, 65,* 85–95.

Crozier, W. R., & Hostettler, K. (2003). The influence of shyness on children's test performance. *British Journal of Educational Psychology, 73,* 317–328.

Crozier, W. R., & Perkins, P. (2002). Shyness as a factor when assessing children. *Educational Psychology in Practice, 18,* 239–244.

Darwin, C. (1872). *The expression of emotions in man and animals.* New York, NY: Philosophical Library.

Dealey, C. E. (1923). Problem children in the early school grades. *Journal of Abnormal Psychology & Social Psychology, 18,* 125–136.

Decker, L. E., & Rimm-Kaufman, S. E. (2008). Personality characteristics and teacher beliefs among pre-service teachers. *Teacher Education Quarterly, 35,* 45–64.

Degnan, K. A., & Fox, N. A. (2007). Behavioral inhibition and anxiety disorders: Multiple levels of a resilience process. *Development and Psychopathology, 19,* 729–746.

Deng, Q., Trainin, G., Rudasill, K. M., Kalutskaya, I., Wessels, S., Torquati, J., & Coplan, R. J. (2015). *Preservice teachers' strategies and attitudes toward hypothetical shy, exuberant, and typical children.* Manuscript submitted for publication.

Ding, X., Liu, J., Coplan, R. J., Chen, X., Li., D., & Sang, B. (2014). Self-reported shyness in Chinese children: Validation of the Children's Shyness Questionnaire and exploration of its links with adjustment and the role of coping. *Personality and Individual Differences, 68,* 183–188.

Doey, L., Coplan, R. J., & Kingsbury, M. (2014). Bashful boys and coy girls: A review of gender differences in childhood shyness. *Sex Roles, 70,* 255–266.

Evans, M. A. (2001). Shyness in the classroom and home. In W. R. Crozier & L. E. Alden (Eds.), *International handbook of social anxiety: Concepts, research and interventions relating to the self and shyness* (pp. 159–183). Westport, CT: John Wiley & Sons Ltd.

Evans, M. A., & Bienert, H. (1992). Control and paradox in teacher conversations with shy children. *Canadian Journal of Behavioural Science, 24,* 502–516.

Eysenck, H. J. (1947). *Dimensions of personality.* Oxford, England: Kegan Paul.

Fantuzzo, J. W., Stovall, A., Schachtel, D., Goins, C., & Hal, R. (1987). The effects of peer social initiations on the social behavior of withdrawn maltreated preschool children. *Journal of Behavior Therapy and Experimental Psychiatry, 18,* 357–363.

Farmer, T. W., Hamm, M. M., & Hamm, J. V. (2011). Revealing the invisible hand: The role of teachers in children's peer experiences. *Journal of Applied Developmental Psychology, 32,* 247–256.

Finn, J. D., Pannozzo, G. M., & Voelkl, K. E. (1995). Disruptive and inattentive-withdrawn behaviour and achievement among fourth graders. *The Elementary School Journal, 95,* 421–434.

Fox, N. A., Henderson, H. A., Marshall, P. J., Nichols, K. E., & Ghera, M. M. (2005). Behavioral inhibition: Linking biology and behavior within a developmental framework. *Annual Review of Psychology, 56,* 235–262.

Fox, N. A., Henderson, H. A., Rubin, K. H., Calkins, S. D., & Schmidt, L. A. (2001). Continuity and discontinuity of behavioral inhibition and exuberance: Psychophysiological and behavioral influences across the first four years of life. *Child Development, 72,* 1–21.

Freud, S. (1924). The dissolution of the Oedipus complex. *Standard Edition, 19,* 172–179.

Freud, S. (1938). *An outline of psychoanalysis.* London, England: Hogarth.

Freud, S. (1964). An outline of psycho-analysis. In J. Strachey (Ed. and Trans.), *The standard edition of the complete psychological works of Sigmund Freud* (Vol. 23, pp. 141–207). London, England: Hogarth Press. (Original work published 1940)

Furman, W., Rahe, D. F., & Hartup, W. W. (1979). Rehabilitation of socially withdrawn preschool children through mixed-age and same-age socialization. *Child Development, 50,* 915–922.

Gazelle, H. (2006). Class climate moderates peer relations and emotional adjustment in children with an early history of anxious solitude: A child x environment model. *Developmental Psychology, 42,* 1179–1192.

Gazelle, H. (2008). Behavioral profiles of anxious solitary children and heterogeneity in peer relations. *Developmental Psychology, 44,* 1604–1624.

Gazelle, H. H., & Ladd, G. W. (2003). Anxious solitude and peer exclusion: A diathesis–stress model of internalizing trajectories in childhood. *Child Development, 74,* 257–278.

Goldsmith, H. H., Lemery, K. S., Buss, K. A., & Campos, J. J. (1999). Genetic analyses of focal aspects of infant temperament. *Developmental Psychology, 35,* 972–985.

Gordon, E. M., & Thomas, A. (1967). Children's behavioral style and the teacher's appraisal of their intelligence. *Journal of School Psychology, 5,* 292–300.

Gortmaker, S., Kagan, J., Caspi, A., & Shiva, P. A. (1997). Day length during pregnancy and shyness in children: Results from Northern and Southern hemispheres. *Developmental Psychobiology, 31,* 107–114

Gottman, J., & Declaire, J. (1997). *Raising an emotionally intelligent child: The heart of parenting.* New York, NY: Fireside.

Hampton, F. A. (1927). Shyness. *Journal of Neurology and Psychopathology, 8,* 124–131.

Hamre, B., & Pianta, R. (2001). Early teacher–child relationships and the trajectory of children's school outcomes through eighth grade. *Child Development, 72,* 625–638.

Herbener, E. S., Kagan, J., & Cohen, N. (1989). Shyness and olfactory threshold. *Personality and Individual Differences, 10,* 1159–1163.

Hirvonen, R., Aunola, K., Alatupa, S., Viljaranta, J., & Nurmi, J. E. (2013). The role of temperament in children's affective and behavioural responses in achievement situations. *Learning and Instruction, 27,* 21–30.

Hobbes, T. (1909). *The leviathan,* Oxford, England: Clarendon Press. (Original work published 1651)

Hofmann, S. G., Asnaani, A., Vonk, I. J. J., Sawyer, A. T., & Fang, A. (2012). The efficacy of Cognitive Behavioral Therapy: A review of meta-analyses. *Cognitive Therapy and Research, 36,* 427–440.

Hughes, K., & Coplan, R. J. (2010). Exploring processes linking shyness and academic achievement in childhood. *School Psychology Quarterly, 25,* 213–222.

Johnson, S. (1795). *Dictionary of the English language in miniature.* London, England: G Staffard.

Kabat-Zinn, J. (1990). *Full catastrophe living: Using the wisdom of your body and mind to face stress, pain and illness.* New York, NY: Dell Publishing.

Kagan, J. (1994). *Galen's prophecy: Temperament in human nature.* New York, NY: Basic Books.

Kagan, J., Reznick, J. S., Clarke, C., Snidman, N., & Garcia Coll, C. (1984). Behavioral inhibition to the unfamiliar. *Child Development, 55,* 2212–2225.

Kagan, J., Reznick, J. S., & Snidman, N. (1987). The physiology and psychology of behavioral inhibition in children. *Child Development, 58,* 1459–1473.

Kagan, J., Reznick, J. S., & Snidman, N. (1988). Biological bases of childhood shyness. *Science, 240,* 167–171.

Kallapiran, K., Koo, S., Kirubakaran, R., & Hancock, K. (2015). Effectiveness of mindfulness in improving mental health symptoms of children and adolescents: A meta-analysis. *Child and Adolescent Mental Health, 20,* 182–194.

Kalutskaya, I. N., Archbell, K. A., Rudasill, K. M., & Coplan, R. J. (2015). Shy children in the classroom: From research to educational practice. *Translational Issues in Psychological Science, 1,* 149–157.

Karevold, E., Ystrøm, E., Coplan, R. J., Sanson, A., & Mathiesen, K. S. (2012). A prospective longitudinal study of shyness from infancy to adolescence: Stability, age-related changes, and prediction of socio-emotional functioning. *Journal of Abnormal Child Psychology, 40,* 1167–1177.

Kingsbury, M., Coplan, R. J., & Rose-Krasnor, L. (2013). Shy but getting by? An examination of the complex links between shyness, coping, and socio-emotional functioning in childhood. *Social Development, 22,* 126–145.

Kohlberg, L., LaCrosse, J., & Ricks, D. (1972). The predictability of adult mental health from childhood behavior. In B. B. Wolman (Ed.), *Manual of child psychopathology* (pp. 1217–1284). New York, NY: McGraw-Hill.

Lao, M. G., Akseer, T., Bosacki, S., & Coplan, R. J. (2013). Self-identified childhood shyness and perceptions of shy children: Voices of elementary school teachers. *International Electronic Journal of Elementary Education, 5,* 269–284.

Lewis-Morrarty, E., Degnan, K. A, Chronis-Tuscano, A., Pine, D. S., Henderson, H. A., & Fox, N. A. (2015). Infant attachment security and early childhood behavioral inhibition interact to predict adolescent social anxiety symptoms. *Child Development, 86,* 598–613.

Liu, J., Coplan, R. J., Chen, X., Li, D., Ding, X., & Zhou, Y. (2014). Unsociability and shyness in Chinese children: Concurrent and predictive relations with indices of adjustment. *Social Development, 23,* 119–136.

Locke, J. (1823). An essay concerning human understanding. *The Works of John Locke* (Vol. 2). London, England: Printed for T. Tegg. (Original work published 1689)

Lowenstein, P., & Svendsen, M. (1938). Experimental modification of the behavior of a selected group of shy and withdrawn children. *American Journal of Orthopsychiatry, 8,* 639–654.

Markovic, A., & Bowker, J. C. (2015). Shy but funny? An examination of peer-valued characteristics as moderators of the associations between anxious-withdrawal and peer outcomes during early adolescence. *Journal of Youth and Adolescence, 44,* 833–846.

McClowry, S. G. (2014). *Temperament-based elementary classroom management.* Lanham, MD: Rowman & Littlefield.

McClowry, S. G., Snow, D. L., & Tamis-LeMonda, C. S. (2005). An evaluation of the effects of "INSIGHTS" on the behavior of inner city primary school children. *Journal of Primary Prevention, 26,* 567–584.

McGuire, S., Clifford, J., Fink, J., Basho, S., & McDonnell, A. M. (2003). Children's reactions to the unfamiliar in middle childhood and adolescence: An observational twin/sibling study. *Personality and Individual Differences, 35,* 339–354.

Mead, G. H. (1934). *Mind, self, and society.* Chicago, IL: University of Chicago Press.

Morris, D. P., Soroker, E., & Buruss, G. (1954). Follow-up studies of shy, withdrawn children—I. Evaluation of later adjustment. *American Journal of Orthopsychiatry, 24,* 743–754.

Negreiros, J., & Miller, L. D. (2014). The role of parenting in childhood anxiety: Etiological factors and treatment implications. *Clinical Psychology: Science and Practice, 21,* 3–17.

O'Connor, E. E., Cappella, E., McCormick, M. P., & McClowry, S. G. (2014). Enhancing the academic development of shy children: A test of the efficacy of INSIGHTS. *School Psychology Review, 43,* 239–259.

Online Etymology Dictionary. (n.d.). Retrieved from www.etymonline.com/index.php?term=shy&allowed_in_frame=0

Pérez-Edgar, K., Reeb-Sutherland, B. C., McDermott, J. M., White, L. K., Henderson, H. A., Degnan, K. A., Fox, N. A. (2011). Attention biases to threat link behavioral inhibition to social withdrawal over time in very young children. *Journal of Abnormal Child Psychology, 39,* 885–895.

Pérez-Edgar, K., Schmidt, L. A., Henderson, H. A., Schulkin, J., & Fox, N. A. (2008). Salivary cortisol levels and infant temperament shape developmental trajectories in boys at risk for behavioral maladjustment. *Psychoneuroendocrinology, 33,* 916–925.

Perren, S., & Alsaker, F. D. (2006). Social behavior and peer relationships of victims, bully-victims, and bullies in kindergarten. *Journal of Child Psychology and Psychiatry, 47,* 45–57.

Piaget, J. (1959). *The language and thought of the child*. London, England: Routlege & Kegan Paul.

Pianta, R. C. (1999). *Enhancing relationships between children and teachers*. Washington, DC: American Psychological Association.

Rapee, R. M. (2013). The preventative effects of a brief, early intervention for preschool-aged children at risk for internalising: Follow-up into middle adolescence. *Journal of Child Psychology and Psychiatry, 54,* 780–788.

Rapee, R. M., Kennedy, S., Ingram, M., Edwards, S., & Sweeney, L. (2005). Prevention and early intervention of anxiety disorders in inhibited preschool children. *Journal of Consulting and Clinical Psychology, 73,* 488–497.

Reznick, J. S., Gibbons, J., Johnson, M., & McDonough, P. (1989). Behavioral inhibition in a normative sample. In J. S. Reznick (Ed.), *Perspective on behavioral inhibition* (pp. 25–49). Chicago: University of Chicago Press.

Richards, E. L. (1921). The elementary school and the individual child. *Mental Hygiene, 5,* 707–723.

Rimm-Kaufman, S. E., & Kagan, J. (2005). Infant predictors of kindergarten behavior: Contributions of inhibited and uninhibited temperament types. *Behavioral Disorders, 30,* 331–347.

Robins, L. N. (1966). *Deviant children grown up*. Baltimore, MD: Williams & Wilkins.

Rodgers, A., & Dunsmuir, S. (2015). A controlled evaluation of the "FRIENDS for Life" emotional resiliency programme on overall anxiety levels, anxiety subtype levels and school adjustment. *Child and Adolescent Mental Health, 20,* 13–19.

Rosenberg, A., & Kagan, J. (1987). Iris pigmentation and behavioral inhibition. *Developmental Psychobiology, 20,* 377–392.

Rosenberg, A., & Kagan, J. (1989). Physical and physiological correlates of behavioral inhibition. *Developmental Psychobiology, 22,* 753–770.

Rousseau, J. J. (1984). *A discourse on inequality* (M. Cranston, trans.). London, England: Penguin. (Original work published 1755)

Rubin, D. H, Althoff, R. R., Ehli, E. A., Davies, G. E., Rettew, D. C., Crehan, E. T., Walkup, J. T., & Hudziak, J. J. (2013). Candidate gene associations with withdrawn behavior. *Journal of Child Psychology and Psychiatry, 54,* 1337–1345.

Rubin, K. H., & Both, L. (1989). Iris pigmentation and sociability in childhood: A reexamination. *Developmental Psychobiology, 22,* 1–9.

Rubin, K. H., Nelson, L. J., Hastings, P. D., & Asendorpf, J. (1999). The transaction between parents' perceptions of their children's shyness and their parenting styles. *International Journal of Behavioral Development, 23,* 937–958.

Rubin, K. H., Wojslawowicz, J. C., Rose-Krasnor, L., Booth-LaForce, C., & Burgess, K. B. (2006). The best friendships of shy/withdrawn children: Prevalence, stability, and relationship quality. *Journal of Abnormal Child Psychology, 34,* 143–157.

Rudasill, K. M. (2011). Child temperament, teacher-child interactions, and teacher-child relationship: A longitudinal investigation from first to third grade. *Early Childhood Research Quarterly, 26,* 147–156.

Rudasill, K. M., & Konold, T. R. (2008). Contributions of children's temperament to teachers' judgments of social competence from kindergarten through second grade. *Early Education and Development, 19,* 643–666.

Rudasill, K. M., & Rimm-Kaufman, S. E. (2009). Teacher-child relationship quality: The roles of child temperament and teacher-child interactions. *Early Childhood Research Quarterly, 24,* 107–120.

Rudasill, K. M., Rimm-Kaufman, S. E., Justice, L. M., & Pence, K. (2006). Temperament and language skills as predictors of teacher-child relationship quality in preschool. *Early Education and Development, 17,* 271–291.

Schmidt, L. A., Fox, N. A., Rubin, K. H., Sternberg, E., Gold, P. W., Smith, C. C., et al. (1997). Behavioral and neuroendocrine responses in shy children. *Developmental Psychobiology, 30,* 127–140.

Shortt, A. L., Barrett, P. M., & Fox, T. L. (2001). Evaluating the FRIENDS program: A cognitive-behavioral group treatment for anxious children and their parents. *Journal of Clinical Child Psychology, 30,* 525–535.

Simpson, J. A., & Weiner, E. S. C. (1989). *The Oxford English dictionary* (2nd Ed., Vol. XV). Oxford, England: Clarendon Press.

Smith, A. K., Rhee, S. H., Corley, R. P., Friedman, N. P., Hewitt, J. K., & Robinson, J. L. (2012). The magnitude of genetic and environmental influences on parental and observational measures of behavioral inhibition and shyness in toddlerhood. *Behavioral Genetics, 42,* 764–777.

Spangler Avant, T. L., Gazelle, H., & Faldowski, R. (2011). Classroom emotional climate as a moderator of anxious solitary children's longitudinal risk for peer exclusion: A child × environment model. *Developmental Psychology, 47,* 1711–1727.

Spooner, A. L., Evans, M. A., & Santos, R. (2005). Hidden shyness in children: Discrepancies between self-perceptions and the perceptions of parents and teachers. *Merrill-Palmer Quarterly, 51,* 437–466.

Sullivan, H. S. (1953). *The interpersonal theory of psychiatry.* New York, NY: Norton.

Suomi, S. J. (1991). Uptight and laid-back monkeys: Individual differences in the response to social challenges. In S. J., Suomi, S. E. Brauth, W. S. Hall, & R. J. Dooling (Eds.), *Plasticity of development* (pp. 27–56). Cambridge, MA: The MIT Press.

Swenson, S. (2015). *Teachers' perceptions of their interactions with shy preschool children: A phenomenological study.* Manuscript submitted for publication.

Thomas, A., & Chess, S. (1977). *Temperament and development.* New York, NY: Brunner/Mazel.

Wentzel, K. R. (2002). Are effective teachers like good parents? Teaching styles and student adjustment in early adolescence. *Child Development, 73,* 287–301.

White, L. K., McDermott, J. M., Degnan, K. A., Henderson, H. A., & Fox, N. A. (2011). Behavioral inhibition and anxiety: The moderating roles of inhibitory control and attention shifting. *Journal of Abnormal Child Psychology, 39,* 735–747.

Wickman, E. K. (1928). *Children's behavior and teachers' attitudes.* New York, NY: Commonwealth Fund Publications.

World Health Organization Report on Prevention of Mental Disorders. (2004). *Effective interventions and policy options summary report.* Department of Mental Health and Substance Abuse in collaboration with the Prevention Research Centre of the Universities of Nijmegen and Maastricht.

Index

About the Authors

Robert J. Coplan is a professor in the Department of Psychology at Carleton University and the director of the Pickering Centre for Research in Human Development. His general research interests are in the area of children's social and emotional functioning in educational contexts. However, for over 20 years, most of his research has focused on the development and implications of shyness in childhood. His previous books include *The Development of Shyness and Social Withdrawal* (with Kenneth Rubin, 2010), *Social Development in Childhood and Adolescence: A Contemporary Reader* (with Melanie Killam, 2011), and the *Handbook of Solitude: Psychological Perspectives on Social Isolation, Social Withdrawal, and Being Alone* (with Julie Bowker, 2014). He lives with his wife and two children in Ottawa, Canada.

Kathleen Moritz Rudasill is an associate professor in the Department of Educational Psychology in the College of Education and Human Sciences at the University of Nebraska-Lincoln, and co-director of the Early Development and Learning Lab. A former teacher, her research is focused on children's temperament in educational settings, with particular emphasis on how teachers and parents can work with children's temperament to optimize learning and success. She has published multiple journal articles and chapters on these topics, and this is her first book. She lives with her husband and two children in Lincoln, Nebraska.